Blind **Br**

Brilliant

3% sight 97% attitude

Theresa **Robberts**

Get in touch

Theresa is the perfect inspirational speaker for your event in person and online. For bookings please email her directly on theresa@theresa-robberts.com

To find out more about this researcher, speaker and sports enthusiast you can connect with Theresa on:

Website:	www.theresa-robberts.com
LinkedIn:	www.linkedin.com/in/theresarobberts
Facebook:	www.facebook.com/ Theresa-Robberts-1727058687333322
Twitter:	twitter.com/TheresaRobberts
Instagram:	www.instagram.com/theresarobberts

First published in 2020 by QuickShift Publishing

PO Box 698, Melville

Johannesburg, 2109

ISBN: 978-0-620-88144-9

Copy edited by	Nikki Metz
Cover Illustration by	Shannan Taylor
Cover design by	Callum Jagger
Layout Design by	Megan Barber Designs
Proofreading by	Neville Barber
Published by	QuickShift Publishing

Dedicated to
all my life-changing four-legged
miracles, future and past.

Author's Note

All proceeds of the revenue raised through the sales of this book will be given to a charity selected by the author.

Currently, the chosen charitiy is Blind Cricket England and Wales with a focus of the development of female players.

Every movie has a theme song and *Blind Broken Brilliant* has one too. *Hold On* by Mari Bosman. While writing her book Theresa found encouragement through a special Afrikaans song – *Hou Vas* by Mari Bosman. It lifted her spirits during the most challenging of times. Theresa have asked Mari to write and perform an English version of the song. She hopes that it will inspire her readers in the same way.

Listen to it here: **amazon.com/author/theresarobberts**

Contents

Chapter 1: Shattered

I lifted my tired, aching head. My left eye, the only one with some vision left, caught sight of something precious. A possible escape! Behind the psychiatrist who was droning on in front of me, was a large crack in the window. It was triangular in shape and slightly bigger than my hand. With a few soft taps I'd be able to remove it without breaking the rest of the window and without anyone taking any notice. Why on earth had it not been fixed? Surely those in charge of a mental hospital should realise its potential danger? I knew several fellow 'inmates' who'd seize the opportunity to use it to harm themselves as I wanted to do. I knew even more who'd use it to exact revenge upon a fellow patient or nurse.

Few people would comprehend this grievous way of thinking. But for me, the promise of escape and release that shard of glass brought, far outweighed the potential for injury or getting caught. My mind was working overtime. Patience was key. I'd claim my prize – my new weapon of choice – during the stillness of the night.

It was only three days before Christmas. Here I was; a 43-year-old professional, academic highflier and award-winning motivational speaker – captured like a frightened animal in Weskoppies. I preferred calling it 'Loskoppies' (Loose heads).

Loskoppies is a notorious mental hospital on the outskirts of Pretoria, the capital of South Africa. From afar it looks very inviting. The buildings are set amongst huge trees and lush green gardens, creating a sense of peace and healing. Inside, quite the opposite was true. The buildings, much like the patients, are crying out for care and attention. And neither party is getting it. Neither patient welfare nor building maintenance is a priority at Loskoppies. If you dared venture closer, you'd find some of the buildings almost completely in ruins. Once majestic structures stand empty and desperately lonely, much like the patients trapped inside.

I'm in Ward 26. The double-storey building has around 30 occupants at any given time, with two nurses on duty. It's my third week and by now I've just about given up hope of ever finding any real support within the confines of these walls. Because it's the holiday season, most of the psychiatrists, psychologists and most of the staff are unavailable or off-duty. So not only would many patients not be seeing their loved ones this Christmas, they'd have to wait until mid-January to receive any tangible medical intervention. I'm one of the lucky ones, though, as I have my own room on the ground floor. These rooms are reserved for 'special' cases. And I'm special because with just three per cent sight remaining, I'm considered legally blind. I was a premature baby; as a result my eyes never fully developed and my sight continued to deteriorate over time. From day one I was told that I was not allowed to climb the stairs in any circumstances. I found it quite ironic that they were concerned about me falling down the stairs when, on my first day alone, I had noticed three different places where one could possibly hang oneself. The electric leads lying on the floor whispered to me whenever I walked past, "I am your ticket out! Just a few seconds and you will have eternal peace." Temptation and opportunity were everywhere.

Today marks three-weeks of my stay in this nightmare-turned-reality. My single room has a single bed and one steel cabinet. I try to make it more liveable with gifts like toys that I received from my friends. Thank goodness my mum brought me my own bedding. The institution's bedding reeks of mothballs and desperation. The cabinet is secured with a huge lock provided by my family. This was a great necessity since the only ones out-performing the patients with acts of thievery are the staff. I have the added luxury of a window, but this I'm forced to keep shut at all times. Right beneath my window is an overflowing drain spilling sewage over the grass and paved smoking area below, and I'm not surprised that many of the women on the ward recently became seriously ill. Like most things in Loskoppies, the sewage spill will get attended to only next year.

For the first three days they kept me dressed in something that felt like it came straight from a forties' horror movie. The green and white stripes on the baggy garbs were faded but the name of the hospital was emblazoned proudly on the back. Fortunately by now I am allowed my own clothes. I choose my oldest tracksuit that would be of no great loss if it was stolen.

Later that evening I wait for the corridors to fall silent. As usual, the nurses are nowhere to be seen. As luck would have it, the interview room that holds my precious, tempting piece of glass, is right next to my room. I enter without turning on the light – just one of the advantages of being blind. I knock the window softly … tap tap tap. Instantly, the triangle of glass dislodges and falls down outside. The sound it makes pierces every wall and door of the old building. For a moment I stand frozen, expecting the whole world to be alerted by the crash. I contemplate rushing back to the safety of my room. If they caught me here now, I'd be sent to the ward of hell, Ward 72. I'd be kept in my room like a caged animal and not even be allowed to bathe myself.

But no one heard, no one moved. I sneak down the corridor and out the back door to retrieve my prize. The stench is overwhelming. The triangle of glass lies waiting. It is still intact but I need something smaller or I'll get caught. I put my glass trophy under the leg of a garden chair and press down. Crack! Again, no one hears. I pick up one of the smaller shards. It's about two by two inches with very sharp edges. It's perfect.

Suddenly, I hear the outside door open. Sheila, a fellow inmate, has come outside for a smoke.

"What's that?" she asks, pointing to the glass on the floor.

"Not sure," I lie. "I just heard the noise when I moved the chair."

"Oh my god!" she exclaims. "Someone broke that out of the window! Who could it be?"

"That's scary," I say, with the smaller piece of glass wrapped in my hand behind my back.

"I bet it's that violent woman they took away to 72 this afternoon," Sheila decides. It's too dark for her to see the relief on my face.

For the next hour there is pandemonium as nurses and patients all yammer away about the incident of the broken window.

One very observant young woman mentions that there is still a piece missing. But no one listens. They never do.

I wait until the dust has settled before retrieving my little slice of freedom from where I have hidden it in my pillowcase. Until now I have been able to get hold only of old nails and jagged stones. They were initially sufficient for my needs but had soon lost their effectiveness. I press one of the sharp glass edges against the soft, pale skin on the inside of my upper left arm. With one swift movement I draw a line towards the inside of my elbow. I have underestimated the efficacy of the glass shard. The blood gushes down my arm and within seconds there is a pool of blood on the floor. It scares me; I grab some toilet paper and quickly cover my new wound. It needs lots of urgent care and attention. A lot like me.

I'd heard of people self-harming before and, like many, I thought it was a selfish way to seek attention. I could not have been more wrong. My wounds were private and the scars they left were a great burden of shame. What drives this inexplicable action is the need to escape. It is a form of release. When you have a wound on your arm your attention moves away from the pain in your heart. You enjoy a fleeting moment of freedom.

So how did someone like me, the girl with the warrior heart, end up in a place like this, a horrendous government mental hospital? I'd been coping exceptionally well with a severe visual impairment. Surely any other challenges life threw my way would pale in comparison?

Not quite. I had a much deeper and darker demon to deal with than blindness.

Depression.

With my arm covered in toilet paper bandages, I sit awake through another sleepless night filled with panic and heartache. My thoughts start wandering back, right back to the beginning.

Chapter 2: A premature beginning

After struggling to conceive, my mum unexpectedly became the mother of two boys – just 14 months apart. The second was a difficult birth and although the doctor advised her to consider a hysterectomy, she chose to go on birth control instead. In September of 1974 she and my dad visited her parents. As usual, the visit to the in-laws, better known as a visit to the outlaws, was a very stressful affair.

"I have a splitting headache. Stepmum has been giving me a hard time all day," my mum admitted to my dad when they were finally alone one evening. My dad suggested that the cause of her headache might not be her stepmum but rather a side-effect of the birth-control pills she was on. That weekend my mum skipped a tablet and she and my dad made the most of the fact that her headache was gone. The Universe decided to make the most of it too.

My mum made an appointment with her doctor to arrange for the hysterectomy the following month as he had suggested. It was there that she received the happy news:

"Mrs Robberts, I am sorry, but I don't think we can perform a hysterectomy just yet. You are pregnant ... again."

Exactly seven months later, on the very same day my brother André had been born a mere year ago, my mum was lying in the same hospital, with the very same nurses attending to her. During my brother's difficult and lengthy labour, my mum had told the nurses that should she find herself in the same position a year later, she'd jump from a mountain. The nurses now jokingly asked her, "Can we bring you a mountain, Mrs Robberts?"

In the mid-seventies, hospitals did not have the technology they have today. Because of my weight of four pounds, the doctor was sure I was ready to meet the world. My mum disagreed, because she knew exactly when I had been conceived, but there was no arguing with the good doctor and he decided to induce labour. He managed to get another thing wrong. He had predicted my mum would have her third son.

It was a chilly morning in May 1975 when, in a very basic military hospital in a very small town that used to be called Pietersburg, a tiny baby girl was born. What should have been a cause for celebration, soon turned into a reason to panic. The little girl had been born much too early and a frantic scene unfolded in the maternity ward. Doctors were rushing, nurses were sobbing and the parents were praying. But some babies should come with a warning label. If this little girl had, it would have read: "Caution: contains undisclosed amounts of tenacity." Premature babies born in the seventies were a far greater cause for concern than they are now, thanks to advancements in medical technology.

I was born nine weeks premature and, as a result, my eyes never fully developed. Fortunately, I was also born with bucket-loads of tenacity and a deep-seated desire for independence. Many would argue that I have more guts than brains and that there is a fine line between stubbornness and stupidity, but more about that later ...

As a result of my premature birth, I have an eye condition called retinopathy of prematurity, commonly referred to as ROP. It affects several parts of the eyes. In my case it ruined my retinas, which means I have peripheral vision loss, or what is better known as tunnel vision. (If you're good-looking, please stand in front of me, not beside me.) I also have myopia or near-sightedness. (This means that if you're good-looking and now standing in front of me, please come closer, a lot closer.) To add insult to injury, I also have strabismus and astigmatism. Thanks to the strabismus I can make eye contact at the same time with two people sitting at opposite ends of a room. Yes, while one eye looks left the other looks right – a bit like a love affair gone wrong. Astigmatism means my corneas are asymmetrical, making it hard for me to focus. I've had all kinds of surgical procedures on my eyes and as a result, am now left with about three per cent sight – just enough to get me into trouble. Humour is my crutch. When you can't see much else, it's important to see the funny side of life. Doing so has been a lifesaver for me. Of course, I don't always see the humour in everything, but mostly I do.

When by the age of 16 months I had not crawled or walked properly, my parents took me to see Professor Hennie Meyer, a well-known ophthalmologist. He gave me my first pair of spectacles, kept in place with a thick elastic band. Within two days I was walking. As Prof. Meyer explained, I had not walked or even crawled as I could not see anything to walk or crawl towards.

I had a happy childhood. My parents raised me in exactly the same way they did my brothers. I didn't receive any special treatment just because I had some loss of sight. This was rather tough at times, but it also made me the independent person I am today. My brothers teased and bullied me just like older brothers do, especially my eldest brother Hannes. He teased and I retaliated and we both got into trouble often. Whether it was cycling or skateboarding, playing rugby or cricket, I was always part of the action in some way.

Although I was brought up in a very strict Christian household, our home was always filled with love and we never wanted for anything. Much to my mum's disgust, I turned out to be a typical tomboy and not the spitting image of Shirley Temple she had hoped for. I hated pink and loved blue. I cried when I had to wear a dress and often lost my shoes as I preferred going barefoot.

Playing with boys can exact its toll on any girl. It's even harder when you're stubborn and visually impaired. My brothers and I often played cowboys and crooks. It mostly involved me trying to catch my brother Hannes, who was much faster than I was. On one particular afternoon, though, I thought I had finally been given my chance. For reasons unknown to me, Hannes was running all the way around a big field instead of straight across it. I set off straight across as fast as my little legs could carry me, spurred on by the idea that victory would finally be mine if I could intercept him. It never occurred to me that there had to be a reason he was running around the field. And that it was simply one I couldn't see. But I soon felt it when I ran into a barbed-wire fence at full speed. I was flung back violently as tiny little slivers of my skin stayed behind on the fence.

Thanks to our parents, we saw and experienced so much of what our country had to offer and often went caravanning. I was 13 when we went on holiday to a place near God's Window in the former Eastern Transvaal, today called Mpumalanga. My brothers were going on an outing horseback riding and I, of course, insisted on joining them. I remember that I was dressed in white shorts and a white shirt, not very practical. My mum finally relented but asked the guide to give me the slowest, laziest horse available. Perched on Bruno's back, I couldn't be more proud. The horses were trained and knew the way to the lookout spot. Although Bruno was slow, he was also rather haughty and insisted on taking the lead. Every time someone tried to pass, Bruno simply moved to the side to prevent this. When a lad who joined the group and knew his way around horses decided to charge past to the front, Bruno became very upset and started chasing the offending horse. Finally having caught up with his nemesis, Bruno bit it and reared in victory. I came crashing down into the dust, much to the amusement of my brothers.

Once we reached the lookout point, the horses had some time to rest and after about an hour, we were ready to head back. Not a second after I was back in the saddle in my dust-covered clothes, Bruno decided to gallop off down the path. At the entrance to the lookout point you had to duck underneath a tar pole if you were on horseback. Though I remembered to do so, I misjudged the distance and was smacked bang on the forehead when I lifted my head too soon. My spectacles were in pieces and I was knocked out cold. My brothers, as usual, were hardly worried and instead could not stop laughing. My forehead remained black and blue for two weeks after the incident.

My first school was Prinshof School for the Visually Impaired, in Pretoria. I thrived. I made friends quickly. Not all the girls were impressed with the fact that I liked rugby and would do anything if a dare was involved. Because the school catered for my needs, my visual impairment disappeared. Almost everyone wore thick spectacles and all the books were in large print. At around this time, my dad, my uncle and my granddad started what would become a very successful business in the pest control industry. I was five and very upset that our dining room was their office and, as a result, out of bounds for me. It was my favourite place to play with my brothers' toy cars. The legs of the table and chairs were the imaginary buildings of a city I had created. I spent hours under that table. Fortunately, the business grew fast and the office moved out of our home. I was queen of my city again.

When I was 10, my dad was asked to open a branch in Cape Town. We had to move. The only other school that catered for my needs was in Worcester. My parents didn't want me to go to a school so far out of the city as it meant I would have to attend as a boarder. They feared that being away from home would interfere with my strict Christian upbringing. Several medical and psychological assessments were done. The report from the ophthalmologist said that I would not cope in a mainstream school. The report from the psychologist, on the other hand, said that I would. My parents chose to go the mainstream route.

Chapter 3: Mainstream bullies

I clearly remember the meeting we had with the headmaster of Goodwood Park Primary School in Cape Town.

"Mr and Mrs Robberts, I will make sure Theresa gets all the support she needs," Mr Gerber said reassuringly. Looking back, I think it was probably far easier for him to say what my parents wanted to hear than to admit he had no clue.

My first day at a mainstream school was in April 1985. The first of many shocks was the size of the class. At Prinshof there were 10 of us. At Goodwood Park, 40 children were crammed into one classroom. I remember my teacher, Miss Van Der Westhuizen, quite unceremoniously making me the centre of attention, though it might not have been her intention, by asking me to sit in the front of the class. Unfortunately, even from there, I could not see what was written on the blackboard. I stood up to have a closer look and practically had my nose pressed against the blackboard when a boy blurted out: "Can't you see? Are you blind or what?" Although that was embarrassing enough, Miss Van Der Westhuizen managed to add insult to injury by pointing out to the class that I couldn't see very well and that I wore very special glasses. I know she meant well but word soon spread that the new girl was different and the relentless teasing started. Speckled

Freckle, Specasaurus, Madam Specs-a-lot, were some of the kinder names I was called. But my Coke-bottle glasses were there to stay.

My spectacles were unusually thick and large. They were so heavy, in fact, that I often had blisters on my ears because of the weight at my temples. Our medical aid covered only one pair a year. For a girl like me, this was not nearly enough. I'd often step or sit on them – sometimes actually by accident. My dad would then use insulation tape to fix them, but he never seemed to have the same colour on hand as he had used for the previous repair. I often wore my horror-specs glued together with blue, black and red tape. The blisters on my ears and the permanent red mark on the bridge of my nose were nothing compared to the damaging effect of these glasses on my self-esteem.

My visual impairment was not the only factor that made life at school extremely challenging. My parents and I were followers of a very strict religion and based all their beliefs 100 per cent on a literal interpretation of the Bible. I was not forced into this religion; it was my choice but it was not an easy path. Forget about celebrating Christmas and birthdays as they had bad associations and were considered pagan. While all the other kids sang birthday songs and ate birthday cake, I sat on my own and couldn't participate. Competitive sport or any extra-curricular activities involving time spent with schoolmates were a big no-no. We had to find our friends and any possible sporting activities or hobbies within the faith. As a young child I was taught to stand strong and stay neutral. This meant, much to the disgust of some right-wing teachers, not standing to attention for the school's or our country's anthems. I did not participate in Bible study at school and never went on any Sunday School camps. If my visual impairment did not make me stand out, my religion most certainly did.

My stubborn independent streak reared its ugly head quite early in life. I insisted on cycling to school as my brothers did. I was instructed to cycle on the pavement and was happy with that. It was one way to avoid road accidents. I was pretty good at cycling on the pavement, turning tree roots and rocks into obstacles and ramps on the racecourse in my imagination. The only problem with this was that my bicycle tyres constantly had punctures my dad needed to fix. Every weekend he'd spend his Saturday afternoon fixing my bike's punctures. I always joined him and watched him closely. I knew he'd much rather be doing something else. One such Saturday afternoon I decided that I'd seen my dad do it a thousand times and concluded that it couldn't be too hard. I took my bicycle into the garage and closed the door. It was my first attempt at fixing a puncture and I did not want anyone to know what I was up to until the job had been completed successfully.

I turned the bike upside down just as I'd seen my dad do a thousand times. It was balancing quite easily on the handlebars and seat. Next I had to remove the tyre from the rim. My dad always made sure that the tube was completely deflated and then used the back of a spoon to remove the tyre. It looked easy enough when he did it but proved to be very hard for me. Each time I thought I had just about managed to wedge the spoon between the rim and the tyre, it shot loose. And what does a visually impaired person do when something doesn't seem to be working? You move closer. With my nose hardly an inch away from the wheel, I finally managed to wedge the spoon under the tyre. Then it shot loose with great force and hit me with a loud smack on my nose. I don't know which was worse – the pain, the blood or the humiliation. I did not finish the job but I did clean up the blood and took care of the humiliation by not telling a soul.

My father eventually found a solution that was great for him but awful for me. He fitted my bicycle with 'perma tubes'. They were solid and did not get punctured but they were very heavy and I hated them. They made navigating my imaginary racetrack very difficult so I decided to lighten the load. I did so by taking everything off: mud guards, any unnecessary covers and the brakes. I rode like that for three years without incident or accident. It did give me a dangerous level of confidence when I first tried my hand at riding a motorbike later in life.

I was known as a soft target for testing new pranks at school. Kids would unscrew the wheels of my bike to the extent that it would only take one move for the wheel to come off, and yes 'the wheels did come off'. They knew I couldn't see well enough to fix the bike myself so they watched and laughed as I walked home with my bicycle under one arm and the loose wheel under the other. Though my brothers had shown me some very handy self-defence manoeuvres, all this meant was that the bullying and teasing always happened just outside my reach.

Being bullied was only one of the very many disadvantages of being at a mainstream school. Academically, I entered the world of the unattainable for the first time. At Prinshof I had often been top of my class and very proud of this accomplishment. When I opened my first workbook on day one of mainstream schooling, I could not see the lines. They were a light blue colour on an off-white background. I was used to white pages with dark blue lines. I assumed the pages had margins and that I just couldn't see them, so I started writing where I imagined the margin would be. This did not amuse my teacher as she drew a red margin and informed me that it was my job to draw a margin on every page.

The upside of not seeing very well was that I became quite good at memorising things. Standing up to see what was written on the blackboard meant that I was in the way of the other students, so the less frequently I did so the better. I tried to memorise more information each time. Miss Van Der Westhuizen turned out to be one of my better teachers. At the end of my first year, she convinced the headmaster that I could be moved to the A-class the following year. I was there for all of 20 minutes. The teacher, Mr Burchfield, a very large, very scary, very bearded man, took one look at me and sent me straight to the B-class. "The A-class has no place for children like you. You will only waste our time." A small voice inside of me wanted to shout, "But I deserve to be in the A-class." Instead, I left teary-eyed and terrified of the bearded bully.

Fortunately, I had only kind teachers in all of my classes after that. It made everything a little less daunting, but did not solve my immediate problem: that I simply could not see work on the blackboard and that much of the printed material was illegible to me. I still can't spell properly. When we were taught spelling, the teacher would write a list of words on the blackboard. We would then copy these words into our workbooks to practise and memorise at home. The next day we'd be tested on the words and every time I'd fail miserably. Not because I hadn't studied. In fact, I studied quite hard. But time and time again I had copied the words incorrectly from the blackboard.

At the end of each school year there was a prize-giving ceremony. Each class had several certificates up for grabs and I desperately wanted to win one. Top-of-the-class honours were out for me, but Most Improved Student or Most Eager Student was well within my reach and what I had set my sights on. Most Improved Student was measured by how much your marks had increased from the second to the third term and Most Eager Student was up to the teacher.

I worked extremely hard and managed to up my average by 9.2 per cent. Unfortunately, my classmate Barry managed to increase his marks by 9.4 per cent and he received the Most Improved Student award. I imagined that, because of my disability and the fact that I had to work so much harder than anyone else, I'd at the very least be first in line for Most Eager Student, but it turned out that I was never even in the running. It was awarded to a boy whose parents were close friends with the teacher. When I asked the teacher why I hadn't even been in contention for the prize, he simply said: "You can't have everything, Theresa."

I absolutely loved sports but, because of our faith, wasn't allowed to participate. My visual impairment also meant no one really thought it was a good idea anyway. On the rare occasion that I was allowed to play, I did so with gusto. One afternoon, during our physical education class we were all sitting on the rugby field in a circle playing a game called rotten egg (similar to duck, duck, goose except we used a tennis ball to 'tag' the 'it' player instead of tapping them on the head). One nasty girl put the ball behind my back thinking I would not see. And though I might well not have seen it, I did hear it. I spun around, grabbed the ball and ran like hell.

I knew catching her would be hard, so I did what any reasonably competitive little girl would: I dove. I rugby-tackled her so hard that even my brothers would have been proud. I managed only to grab her leg but she went flying and fell to the ground with a reverberating thud. Her face was covered in the white chalk markings of the rugby field. With her white face and bruised ego she had to be the rotten egg in the middle. She tried gaining sympathy from the PE teacher but was met with a caution instead: "That'll teach you for picking on the blind girl." That day, and a few weeks after, I reigned supreme and enjoyed a little peace and quiet from the bullies.

My parents were never terribly concerned about my academic performance in primary school. When my average dropped from an A at Prinshof to a C at Goodwood Park, it wasn't an issue for them. High school, on the other hand, proved to be a much bigger challenge.

Chapter 4: High school hell

High school can be either some of the best or some of the worst years of your life ... The first two years of high school turned out to be the latter for me. It was an extremely challenging time. It was before Harry Potter, so my spectacles were a spectacle rather than a fashion statement. To add to my misery, I was fitted with braces and orthodontic headgear. My mum also insisted that my skirt hung well below my knees. At every inspection I was addressed not because my skirt was too short, but because it was too long.

According to my classmates, I was more metal than human and thus they dubbed me Robocop. Although outright name-calling became less frequent, something far worse happened: social exclusion. Not being invited, not being picked for a team, not being asked to participate, and being ignored all became the order of the day.

We moved back to Pretoria in 1989. During the school holidays I met and became friends with a few teenagers who all went to Zwartkop High School. When I was given the option of returning to Prinshof, I decided at the last minute that I'd rather attend Zwartkop where I had at least already made a few friends. This turned out to be a not very wise choice. Zwartkop High School was huge and still fairly new as schools go. The meeting my parents and I had with the headmaster, Dr Malan, went much the same way as the one we had had with the headmaster of Goodwood Park. We were promised all the support we'd ever need. "I will discuss Theresa's needs with all my staff," Dr Malan said quite confidently and reassuringly. My mum thanked him. As in many other meetings and appointments that were about me, I was never addressed directly. It was as though I wasn't even present. I was never given the opportunity to comment, ask questions or raise any concerns. It was just not the done thing. And though I am sure Dr Malan did actually tell his staff that a visually-impaired pupil had enrolled at the school, I don't believe the conversation ever went any further than that. No real thought was given nor any practical measures put in place to enable the staff to support me.

The sheer size of the school meant that discipline wasn't really enforced and any complaints about bullying fell on deaf ears. The social exclusion continued and I remember one bullying incident quite clearly. A senior boy was standing on the first floor, leaning over the railing. He snorted and sucked all the phlegm and mucus he could muster from his throat and nostrils, gathering it all in his mouth. As I walked by down below, he spat it out all over my head.

"Bull's-eye!" he shouted in triumph to his mates and anyone who'd listen.

"And she can't event report me because she can't see me" he snickered loudly. This was met with an even louder roar of laughter. Struggling to hold back the tears, I hurried to the nearest bathroom to try washing the gunk from my hair.

As terrible as the bullying was, my biggest problem at Zwartkop was inside the classroom. By this time we had switched from blackboards to transparencies on an overhead-projector. I couldn't see a thing. Though I was given the transparency worksheet after every class so I could copy the work, it was really difficult and the teachers simply weren't equipped to deal with a visually-impaired pupil. I also couldn't copy the work from classmates' workbooks, as this would mean they'd have to loan me their books for the afternoon, and everybody simply had too much homework to do after school. Quite rapidly, I started falling behind with my schoolwork. But supporting me as a visually impaired student really wasn't rocket science … Print the work on white paper and enlarge it to A3 size? For some reason this seemed an impossible ask. The teachers were already struggling with classrooms that were filled to capacity, mostly with ill-disciplined students. I suppose there just wasn't any time.

During an annual visit to Zwartkop, the school inspector came to our mathematics class. All our workbooks were lying on the teacher's table. He randomly selected a few and started paging through them. One of his selections turned out to be mine. It was already October, so most of the students' books were filled almost to capacity. Mine, on the other hand, contained hardly 10 pages of work. The young maths teacher was in a great deal of trouble and I really felt sorry for her. I could hardly blame her or any of my teachers, though, as they'd never been given the tools required to support a pupil like me.

It was only after many months of arguing and begging that the teachers allowed me extra time to complete my tests and exams. And this came with another problem, of course. After each test period, I'd inevitably be late for the next class. Pupils were allowed five minutes to move from one class to the next. You had to make it within that time or suffer the consequences. I often ran late. On one particular day, my next lesson was in a classroom on the other side of the school grounds. The school was built on a slope on the typical rocky, red soil and dust of the Highveld. The only grass the school had planted was on the rugby field. The hill I had to move down had only one narrow set of cement stairs. I knew if I had to wait for the single file of pupils making their way up and down, I'd never get to my class in time. So I did what any visually-impaired girl in my position would do: I tried to run down the rocky red hill instead. No sooner had I taken my first step than I tripped and started somersaulting down the hill. At the bottom, I got to my feet and rushed off before the clouds of red dust had time to settle. The embarrassment of my fall was far greater than any injuries I might have sustained, which is why I did not stop until I had reached the safety of my next class. At the door, I looked down and saw little streams of mud forming as the blood and dust painted a map down my legs. The teacher took one look at me and promptly dismissed me with permission to go and clean up.

What high school looks and feels like might change over time, but people's behaviour, in essence, remains the same. And if you're different in any way, you can almost count on being excluded. There's always the 'in crowd' and the 'out crowd'. I was even too out for the out crowd. Or any crowd for that matter. I didn't really have all that much going for me. My skirt was too long. My braces were too ornate, and to top it all off, my glasses were too thick. Though I was relatively intelligent, I could hardly prove as much so couldn't even join the nerds at break time. For the most part, I assume people thought me rather dense. I couldn't even do well in typing. Not fitting in anywhere and not being able to progress academically, left me a very quiet and very frustrated young girl. Somewhere, something had to give.

Back then, state nurses used to make their rounds at schools to vaccinate and check basic health of all the pupils. On the odd occasion, this would include a visit by an optometry team. At first, this was great news. We were about to miss geography and that in itself was a triumph. Mrs Appel, the geography teacher, was a mad woman with neither the patience nor the knowledge to deal with anyone who couldn't do map work.

Our class of 40 14-year-olds was squeezed into a small room. Two middle-aged women, looking dull as soup bones, sat behind the desk going through a pile of files. They called out our names to check that everyone was present. Surprisingly, no one had taken the opportunity to sneak out for a smoke break or an illicit snog.

The files were stacked alphabetically and, even from a distance, I could see which one was mine: the really thick one towards the bottom. While almost everyone's files contained perhaps a page or two, mine was like an encyclopaedia. To my absolute horror I realised what would be happening next. Each pupil would have to read the eye-chart out loud in front of the rest of the class. I was mortified and felt like a lamb to the slaughter. Most of my classmates had near-perfect eyesight. I, on the other hand, could hardly see the first two letters on the chart. I could already hear the laughter and the muttering, see the pointing and feel the mocking behind my back. I wanted the earth to swallow me whole. I was going to be thrown to the lions and the spectators were going to love every minute of it.

Having the surname Robberts meant that I'd meet my fate only after 24 other students had had the chance to display the glory of their 20/20 vision. Unnoticed, I snuck over to the desk where the old soup bones sat.

"Ma'am, is there any chance I could sit this one out? I had an eye test only a few weeks ago."

"No, it's compulsory," said the taller of the two soup bones sternly. "Ma'am, have you seen my file? If I have to do this, please can I do it in private?"

"No, this is the room that we were allocated and it would be a waste of our time," said the short, round one.

I was ordered back to my seat in no uncertain terms. I slumped back into my chair and felt the tears well up in my eyes.

"Theresa Robberts!"

It was my turn. The two women whispered to each other as they flipped through my impressive file.

"Stand behind the line."

I did as I was told. I looked around. All of a sudden everyone had gone dead quiet. All eyes were on me as I started reading the chart.

"E," I paused.

"F, P,

T, O, Z,

L, P, E, D."

The fogies stood up.

I continued.

"P, E, C, F, O."

I picked up the pace.

"E, D, F, C, Z, P."

I did not stop. I did not breathe until I had read the last row below the red line.

For a few seconds, time stood still. The tall soup bone jumped up, threw her arms in the air and shouted,

"Praise the Lord, the child can see! Praise the Lord, it's a miracle!"

I looked straight at the two women who had thrown me to the lions and said: "No ma'am, it's not a miracle; it's called memory."

Being number 25 on the list meant that I had ample time to memorise the letters, which I did. The lions now became my allies. My classmates were cheering, clapping and laughing.

Later that same week our class had to make an oral presentation to the entire school. It was a group project and we had to address a specific topic. As no one else was willing, I stepped up to the plate. It was a boring presentation about the possibility of a population explosion. My audience was bored and my nerves got the better of me. I stopped and hesitated.

For a few moments the assembly hall was filled with the most deathly silence. I gave up on the presentation I had prepared and gave the following speech instead. My voice was shaking but I used this to my advantage.

"Yes, my voice is shaking, but yours would be too if you knew what I know. According to statistics, white South Africans are a dying species." Now I had their attention. "White families have, on average, one or maybe two kids. That is not enough to grow a nation. You need more to grow a nation. My advice, if you want the Afrikaner nation to be around for some time, is that you better get out there and start reproducing." With that, I left the stage.

The kids loved it and I got a standing ovation, but I also got into a lot of trouble. The powers that be decided I would not do any presentations on behalf of my class, or any group, ever again.

Mathematics was one of my favourite subjects but it was also the subject I started battling with most due to my poor eyesight. I remember failing geometry tests by the dozen, not because I did not understand the work, but simply because I copied the work down incorrectly from the overhead projector or the blackboard. By the end of grade nine, I was almost certain I was going to fail maths. I also never stood a chance in typing as I wasn't allowed something as simple as being able to use a stand to position the book from which I had to type closer to my face. As a result, when doing a speed test, I'd have to pick up the book, memorise the sentence, put down the book, and type whatever I could remember. I had to repeat that process for every sentence of the test. Regardless of how accurate my typing was, I never finished on time. I was lucky if I made it even halfway through. I was the only pupil in my grade who managed to score an H for typing on her report card.

My overall average was a D. Although this was good enough for a pass, if you failed more than two subjects, you had to repeat the year. In my case it wasn't really a question of if – rather which. Which subjects would I fail? Geography was an absolute nightmare, mostly because of the intricate map work, which constituted a large percentage of the overall geography mark. To pass geography, I had to get an A for theory. But thanks to my map work, that A became an E. I hated having to study so hard for such a ridiculous and skewed average. Biology and science posed much the same problem as I failed miserably when in the sketches. My eyesight was not an issue when it came to history and languages and I excelled in these subjects. Until my grade nine final exam, that is.

On the day of our Afrikaans exam I sat confidently waiting for my paper. When it landed on my desk I nearly burst into tears. It was printed in a very small font, in a light grey colour – similar to old invoices printed from very old computers. It even had perforated edges with holes along the sides. I was completely illegible to me. My hand was shaking as I raised it.

"Ma'am, I cannot read this print," I said quietly to the exam supervisor, my voice shaking.

"Why not?" she asked with a frown.

"I am visually impaired," I explained. This teacher did not teach any of my subjects so she was not aware of my problem.

"I will need it in a darker and larger print."

"Well, I can't do that, I need to stay here. Your Afrikaans teacher should have done this before you sat the exam."

"Ma'am, please can you get help from the administration office? Please give them a call." My voice was still shaking but no longer soft.

"No, it's not my responsibility, I am only here to supervise and you are disrupting this exam."

I felt like I could no longer hold back the tears and envisaged a very embarrassing situation unfolding. I was ready to explode. Instead of tears, an anger that had been simmering deep inside for a very long time manifested itself. I found courage that I never knew existed, stood up, turned to the teacher and said, "When I enrolled in this school, Dr Malan promised support from every staff member in this school and that includes you."

My legs were like jelly but my voice was calm, firm and strong. "If you don't want to give me this support then I will have to go and ask him why his promise is not being kept."

With this I made my way to the door.

"No, wait! I'll call the office and consult your teacher," said the supervisor before I reached the door.

A new paper was arranged and I wrote the exam later that afternoon.

The grade nine final exams caused me such anxiety that my immune system took a beating and, as a result, a sty formed in my eye. It multiplied within days and soon I could not open my eyes at all because of the swelling. For once, a teacher took action. Mrs Matthews, my mathematics teacher, suggested that I do the exam orally. What a triumph! I got an A for mathematics and you can imagine my joy as this turned things around. I passed through the hell that was grade nine.

I was exhausted from studying until the wee hours of the morning, day after day, just to pass. I approached my parents and they agreed that it would be much better for me to return to Prinshof to complete high school.

Chapter 5: The new normal

It was such a relief being back at a school that catered for my needs. Though the schooling system and subjects were exactly the same, the textbooks came in large print and there were no more inaccessible blackboards and overhead projectors. The teachers were well-informed and responsive to pupils' academic needs. The best thing about being at Prinshof was that my visual impairment all but disappeared. Because everyone had similar issues it was as though they cancelled each other out. No more bullying, teasing or social exclusion. For once, my efforts did not go unrewarded and my average mark increased by more than 25 per cent.

Romance was now firmly on the cards. My visual impairment was no longer an issue and this gave me newfound self-confidence. Stephen was my first boyfriend. The romance had to be embarked upon in secret because my parents, with their strict religious ways, would never allow anything of the kind. Our first date was at the monthly school movie-night. "I could get used to this," I thought to myself. After the movie, we went for a walk. Stephen was looking for an opportunity to take things a little further but I made it very difficult for him.

"Are you cold?" he asked.

"No," I said.

“Would you like my jacket?”

“No, thank you” I replied.

After several failed attempts at finding an excuse to hold me, Stephen resorted to the direct approach.

“Ah well, then I’ll just hold you anyway.” He held me in his arms and we kissed. My feelings were a mixture of excitement, guilt and relief. I was relieved that I had just avoided the label of ‘sweet sixteen and never been kissed’ with only a few weeks to spare. I was experiencing the chemistry between a boy and a girl for the first time, but to be honest, I wasn’t that impressed and couldn’t understand what the hype was all about.

But the overwhelming emotion I felt was guilt. According to my beliefs and upbringing, what we had just done was reserved for people who were about to get married and, more importantly, you engaged in these acts only with someone of the same faith. When my mum fetched me from school later that evening, I told her I was tired and lay down in the back of the car. I was worried sick she’d notice something different about me or, just by looking at my face, would be able to tell what had happened.

Over the next few months, Stephen and I made excuses and found ways to be alone together. He was a true gentleman and things never went further than kissing. I was young and in love and truly believed he was The One. I even tried to convince him to join our faith. Fortunately, he didn’t, but the day he declined was also the day I ended our relationship.

Stephen was a year older than me and once he left school we had hardly any contact. Our relationship did make me braver and more confident, however, and in my final school year I often flirted with, and made passes at, boys, but never entered any kind of relationship again. My teenage experiences with romance were fun, but they weren't fulfilling and I always felt as if something was missing.

I still wasn't allowed to participate in any sport that would require me to stay after school, but I was allowed to take part in public speaking competitions. My first attempt was a disaster. We were allowed to wear smart clothes instead of our school uniform. I liked the idea but, since this was a first for me, I had no idea that none of the pupils ever actually did dress up. On the night, I was the only one not in school uniform. It would have been fine, except that I was dressed like a nun, with massive, plastic, eighties-style earrings. I'm eternally grateful the event was never recorded because the only thing more catastrophic than my outfit was my speech.

My topic of choice was why abortion is wrong, and I supported a pro-life argument. It was an acceptable topic for the time and hardly taboo. But I forgot half of my speech, stumbled over my words, and mixed up a lot of my facts and information. For the duration of my speech, I stood rooted behind the lectern like a robot and did not make good use of the microphone. Afterwards I was so embarrassed that I did not want to try it ever again. But then things changed and, under the watchful eye and guidance of Mrs Van Pletson, my English teacher, I started developing what turned out to be a natural talent for public speaking.

My friends loved their sport and, I have to admit, I was sometimes very jealous of them. The girls in my class were excellent at netball. They would play matches against other non-mainstream schools, one of which was the School for the Deaf. The two teams got on well off the court, but on-court it was all guns blazing. Using your opponent's disability to your advantage was very common. I was told that in netball, communication with your fellow team members is very important. The deaf girls simply pointed to the person they wished to pass the ball to, since our girls would not be able to spot this. Our girls would say the name of the person they planned to pass the ball to and simply hold a hand in front of the deaf girl so she that could not lip-read what was said. It was all done in good spirit.

Attending Prinshof for my three final school years was amazing, but certainly not without incident or accident. My parents told me in no uncertain terms that I would not be allowed to attend the matric farewell dance. "Bad associations spoil useful habits," they used to quote from the Bible. As the time grew closer, we somehow managed to change their minds. I was allowed to go, as long as my brother, André, accompanied me. I did not mind at all. We got along well and all I had wanted was to share the experience with my classmates. My mum obtained the services of a dressmaker to help with my dream red dress. It had a flared skirt consisting of several layers of red, shiny fabric, netting and black lace. When my mum fell ill in the weeks leading up to the event she was not able to oversee the final product delivered by the dressmaker who managed to get the layers all wrong. What was meant to be on the inside, ended up on the outside. Funnily enough, this did not bother me much. Unlike most girls, I was not hung up on the dress. And the fact that my classmates could not see the mistake made things easier – one of the many advantages of having visually-impaired friends.

When everyone in your group is visually impaired, there's plenty of opportunity to master the art of pranking. We somehow never ran out of ideas and loved trying out new tricks. Mealtimes with fellow 'blindies' could be such fun and chicken was the perfect ingredient for a prank. You'd gobble up your piece of chicken and then leave the bones on your neighbour's plate. More often than not, they'd only realise they were second-hand sucked-on bones when it was too late. Ice cubes were another favourite. When you can't see what you've been presented with, wrestling an ice-cube with a knife and fork can turn into a very messy, very confusing affair. But we were all naturally prone to embarrassing situations so a well-developed, albeit 'interesting', sense of humour came with the territory.

Once such rather embarrassing situation occurred when one of the boys entered puberty. No one informed the poor lad of the changes his body would be going through. When hair appeared in strange places, he thought it best not to tell anyone and just get rid of the offending growth … He shaved off everything, which would have been fine and well, until he patted on some aftershave. The burn was so bad that the housemother had to soak his privates in milk.

Chapter 6: The world was my oyster

Growing up in a strict religious household did have its advantages. South Africa was going through many changes and turbulence, especially during the '90s. It wasn't really an issue for us as we were taught to see all races as equal, which was unusual for a white Afrikaans family at the time. Throughout my childhood we often had people of colour visit us in secret and we met folks from different cultures and all corners of the globe at international conventions. During one particular convention held in Pretoria in 1992, my mum hosted a braai (barbecue) at our home for a Swedish delegation. My brother, André, our friend Justin and I were fascinated and loved it. That evening, while driving home after dropping the delegation at the airport, we all decided that we wanted to travel abroad. André and Justin did so the following year and visited countries like Sweden and the UK.

For me, it became a dream to travel. When I was in my final school year, I asked my parents if I could go on a Contiki tour once I had saved enough money. I told them many of my friends were interested in joining me and even if they all backed out, I would still go. I'm not sure if they thought I'd never be able to raise the funds or it was just a phase I was going through, but much to my surprise and delight, they said yes. I immediately sprang into action.

At school I sold Chelsea buns each Friday. I'd buy them at the local bakery the afternoon before and somehow managed to lug them all to school with me the next day. By first break, they were all sold out. As it turned out, I had a natural talent for writing essays and orals and offered these services to fellow students at a price. Once I left school I started my own silk-screen printing business and took a part-time job as a receptionist at my dad's firm. I had to turn down many invites to movies and nights out to save money for my dream. I also did not indulge in things like new clothes or any of the other luxuries some of my friends did. I was so focused. I even drew diagrams and stuck them on the office wall to monitor my progress.

In 1995 the big day came. My mum accompanied me to the travel agent to book my five-week tour of 14 countries in Europe. I can remember how proud I felt. Even the cocky young travel agent, who was sitting behind his desk smoking, could feel my excitement. Though I am sure my mum was worried, she shared in my excitement and was every bit as proud of my achievement as I was. After we'd bought the ticket, she took me out for a slice of cheesecake to celebrate. As we were enjoying this treat, she said: "What you have accomplished here is no mean feat. You can be very proud. You set a goal, you worked hard and you achieved it. If you can do this, you will achieve much in life."

The trip to Europe was so much more than anything I had ever imagined it could be. I had a daily budget of R10 and yet felt like a queen. As expected, none of my friends was able to join me, but going on my own was the best thing that could have happened. All decisions, big or small, were mine to make.

I had a bite at the cherry of independence and I was hooked for life.

At 19, I was by far the youngest and most naive person on the tour. I did not drink alcohol unless it was free. Though it wasn't a priority on my budget, I did seem to have more fun than most. Every day was a new experience, a new country or culture and a new memory. I was even more in awe of Contiki themselves. I felt they were a company in the business of making dreams come true and decided there and then that this was the career for me. I wanted to be a tour guide and I wanted to work for this company.

Our tour started in London. I was very nervous and remember calling my dad from a phone booth just to tell him I was about to board the bus. We set off for France. Our first night was in Paris. We enjoyed a Parisian meal and then a walk through the red-light district. Before that I had not even known what a red light district was. I soon learnt it had three main attractions: sex shops, sex shows and bars. I was terrified and thought someone would offer me drugs at any moment, but that never happened. If I knew then that I would, in future, frequent similar places, I would have died on the spot.

From Paris we travelled to the south of France. Monte Carlo was my favourite place. I loved sitting in a pub where so many famous people had been before – Buddy Holly, Elvis Presley and all the Formula One champions. My favourite piece of memorabilia in the pub was a huge South African flag celebrating our Rugby World Cup victory that same year. I had a Springbok T-shirt, which turned out to be quite popular with the foreigners, except for one occasion. We were at the Oktoberfest in Munich when a group of rude and unruly men surrounded me and started shouting: "Apartheid! Apartheid!" They would not let me go until some of the bigger guys in our group intervened and came to my rescue.

In the middle of this whirlwind adventure, we arrived at the Greek island of Corfu. We'd remain there for four days, which was twice as long as any of our other stays. As we drove by coach to our campsite, Mel, the tour guide, told us of an age-old tradition that would be of interest to the ladies in the group. On the third day of our trip, we'd be exploring the island by boat and would be stopping at several secluded beaches. "We'll also make a stop at a very famous cliff," Mel said beaming. "The first lady to jump off wins a T-shirt and a bottle of bubbly." That sounded like me, I thought. Then she added, "Of course, ladies, you have to do this in the nude." Scrap that one, I thought. Not something for a good Christian girl like me.

On the recommendation of a friend, I splashed out on a paragliding experience on our first day. My tent-mate Rose, another South African lass from the East Rand, and I decided to do it together. We were strapped into a harness on the jetty and off we went. It was truly breath-taking. I was at the front and felt that my harness was uncomfortable. I managed to push it from my hips to my thighs, which resulted in me toppling over slightly. The position was awkward but felt much more comfortable, and so I remained, with my bum in the air. What I hadn't taken into consideration (even then), was my lack of distance perception. We were nearing the end of our flight and they started lowering the parachute. I was sure we were still quite far from the water. After swallowing what felt like the half of the Mediterranean Sea, I realised I was wrong.

Greece, and especially the Greek islands, will do funny things to anyone's inhibitions. Come day three, I was solidly into the island spirit. I even started considering the cliff jump competition. Not because it was daring but purely for financial reasons. My budget was tight and, by day three, my money for my stay in Corfu was all dried up. I had not yet bought a souvenir and had no money for drinks on our boat trip. That settled it then. I made sure I was the first girl up the cliff. Getting to the top was hard. Once we got to the top I told the bloke who helped me, "Turn around Troy, and please face the other way." I didn't want him to see me naked even though there was a boatful of tourists watching from below.

I had everything planned: In one quick move, I'd slip out of my demure one-piece swimsuit; I'd keep my flip-flops on (of course); while I was jumping, I'd pull my knees up towards my chest to cover all my lady bits, and as soon as I hit the water I'd redress and, voila! At first, everything went to plan. Mid-air, however, I realised that the water was much further down than my eyes had led me to believe. I could literally count the seconds. Because I had pulled my knees up during the jump, my body tilted backwards which meant that when I hit the water, I had an instant enema and my lower back hit the water with great force. The pain was so intense that all thoughts of getting dressed in a flash were gone. I drifted on the water, face-up, with every bit of my up-to-now chaste body exposed.

Fortunately, the pain subsided and I made a full recovery with more than enough time left to enjoy my well-earned bubbly and to wear my T-shirt with pride. It was not the ideal souvenir for a proper Christian girl to take home. On it were 16 couples in 16 different sex positions, with the words:

Same shit, different day. I did not care. I had earned it and would wear it. It mysteriously disappeared a few days after I arrived home.

We also visited Austria, Germany and Switzerland, where we took the Cog Railway to Jungfrau for a day of skiing. Like many things on this trip, it would be a first for me. The skis were even longer than they looked on television. Standing at the top of the beginners' hill, I had great trouble putting them on and then found it even more difficult to turn around and face the right way to go down the hill. Before I could turn around properly, I started sliding down the hill. And thus my first experience skiing was going downhill backwards with copious amounts of frenetic screaming for added sound effects. I wasn't too far from the bottom of the hill when my skis crossed over one another and I did a couple of backward somersaults before landing, bum in the air, head in the snow.

Italy was one of my favourite places on the tour. I was given many free drinks and told it was because of my long, blonde hair. Wearing an Italian football shirt must have helped as well. The attention I received from the Italian men was very flattering. They seemed to understand English quite well until I said "No!" One evening in Rome, one such gentleman bought me a drink and then invited me to a nearby club where he promised the music would be brilliant. A very naive me agreed. Fortunately, some of the girls on the tour overheard the conversation and followed us. After a few minutes of walking, there were no clubs and only dark alleys. The girls stepped in, and on the way back to our original club, gave me a thorough telling-off for being so irresponsible.

One of the most beautiful places we visited was the Isle of Capri off the coast of Sorrento. We were supposed to go on a trip to the Blue Grotto, a sea cave on the coast of the island, but because of a storm the previous night, our excursion was cancelled and our money refunded. We now had a free day and a pocketful of change to spend on the Isle of Capri. Whatever would we do?

Rose and I decided to rent a scooter and spend the day discovering the island. It was stunning. When we reached the other side of the island I asked her to stop. "Rose," I said confidently. "I paid for half the rental of the scooter so I should drive the rest of the way."

"No way!" she exclaimed in disbelief. "I am not getting on the back of that bike with you driving."

"That's fine," I said calmly. "Guess you'll just have to walk then." I got on the scooter and drove off.

I drove around the block and stopped next to her. "Come on, get on," I said with a smile. She did and we drove on without incident – at least none that I could see. I loved it and shouted like Al Pacino in a scene from *Scent of a Woman*, "Speak to me son! One o'clock, two o'clock!" Rose could only yell in disbelief.

"Don't blame me, Charlie. I can't see!" I again quoted from the movie with a cheeky grin.

We made it back to the rental office in one piece. I was soaring on adrenaline, but for some reason Rose was as white as a sheet. Poor girl, maybe all the fresh air had been a bit much for her.

The Netherlands was the last country on our tour. Amsterdam was amazing and the Dutch people were very friendly. I didn't return to London with our tour group, though. A friend of mine had married a Dutchman and had been living in the Netherlands for a few years. I had arranged to visit them for a few days. I had a small loft room in their home in Bergen op Zoom. Nadine and her husband, Don, were very hospitable and I loved my stay with them. They listened to all my stories of my European adventure. I specifically told them how proud I was that I had not been drunk even once. On the coach we had what was called 'The Spew List'. Everyone who was sick after drinking too much made the list.

"At the end of the tour, my name was the only one not on the list," I said, very proud of myself. That afternoon, Don suggested that we play cards, with the loser of each game having to down a shot of vodka. "I'm in!" I shouted excitedly. I was great at card games and therefore had nothing to fear.

It all started off very well. I won almost every game. I did not take note of the fact that the vodka was kept in the kitchen, and not where we were playing cards. Each time a shot had to be poured, Don went to the kitchen and came back with the shot glass filled. I was surprised that Nadine held her liquor so well since, by that time, she had had several shots but did not look inebriated at all. After a long winning streak, a sudden change took place. I started losing, not one, not two, but many games in a row – resulting in many vodka shots downed. Thankfully, Nadine and Don called it a day and I stood up to go and watch television. It was the first episode of *Friends* that I had ever seen. I loved it! But I started feeling rather tired and could not stop myself from desperately wanting to lie down. It suddenly occurred to me that this wasn't very good manners and that if I needed to lie down, I should do so on my bed in my own room. I tried to get up but my legs simply wouldn't move. Neither would my arms. I couldn't get any of my body parts to cooperate. I was paralysed and felt utterly embarrassed. To make matters worse, I was starting to feel rather ill and knew what was coming next. Luckily, Nadine saw my predicament and helped me to the bathroom. For the first time, I was sick from drinking too much. Don had to carry me to my room. It was around three in the afternoon. I passed out cold and woke up again only 24 hours later.

That evening, Don and Nadine confessed. "Our glasses were filled with water, not vodka," Don said with a mischievous grin.

"Nadine, that's why you did so well." I thought out loud.

"Our problem was the fact that you never lost. We had to cheat with the cards, too."

"Sies, Nadine!" I exclaimed.

"We thought you'd bragged just a little too much," smirked Don, still very pleased with himself.

Many years would pass before I ever touched vodka again.

Chapter 7: Out of reach

Being back home after this life-changing trip was hard. It wasn't just a case of post-holiday blues. My taste of independence left me craving more. I also found that my friends tired quickly of my travel talk and I had no-one with whom to share my newfound joy. From my research it was clear that my South African passport was not exactly a boon when it came to looking for employment abroad. My dream of becoming a tour guide in Europe was not to be. I also learnt that to become a city tour guide in South Africa was quite expensive. The cheaper option was to become a field guide. When I saw an advertisement for a two-week course in Hoedspruit on a game farm, I jumped at the opportunity. It was well within my budget and I truly believed a course like this would open doors for me. I scraped together the last of my savings and enrolled immediately. They did not seem concerned at all by my visual impairment and perhaps this alone should have set off warning bells. But the fact that it did not bother them convinced me even more that this was a totally legitimate endeavour.

The great outdoors isn't really the best place for someone who is visually impaired. By their very nature, many things are naturally camouflaged and the outdoors can become a veritable nightmare. We were asked to identify more than 100 trees just by looking at either branches or trees. There was no way I could tell them apart, not even when I resorted to tasting the leaves. We had only a couple of hours each night to study but no electric lighting. I ended up sitting in the loo with my books since it was the only place with sufficient lighting for me to see.

One evening, after a particularly long and hot day out in the veld, we were sitting around the campfire. I was exhausted and rested my head in my hands with my elbows on my knees. I was wearing a pair of jeans and did not see or feel the scorpion clambering up my leg. I placed my elbow right on top of the scorpion and received an almighty sting.

"Aaaaaaahh!" My rather deafening scream pierced the silence. At first I thought it was a hot ember from the fire but when I inspected my leg I could see I wasn't burnt. The sting hardly left a mark but the pain was excruciating and would not subside. The glands in my armpits were swollen almost immediately. The course facilitators had very little sympathy for me and simply stated that the nearest doctor was much too far away for them to be able to do anything. I was told to sleep it off. Instead I spent the night vomiting and had a severe headache. But I survived.

I failed the course and later also learnt that the game farm that facilitated it was neither registered nor an accredited service provider. I guess I should have seen that one coming.

I still hungered for a career in tourism. My next port of call was the airline industry. In 1997 I enrolled at Birnam Business College for a six-month course after which, they claimed, I would have: SAA Fares 1, Galileo and a diploma in travel and tourism. My mum and I met up with a college representative and the usual promises were made. Of course the college could accommodate a visually-impaired student. Top students are guaranteed a future within the airline industry ... I should have known by now that promises like these hardly ever materialised, but I was so desperate for a career in tourism that I chose to believe her.

The next six months were extremely challenging. The study material was inaccessible because of the small text size. I used a magnifying glass but this only hurt my eyes and didn't help much. The maps provided were of a poor quality but I was informed that we were not allowed to enlarge them or make darker copies. My determination to forge a career in tourism helped me find solutions to any obstacles I encountered. I took each map and used felt-tipped pens to colour each country a different colour. I marked each river, each city, each mountain and each major tourist attraction. Then I used every ounce of willpower to memorise each map. During my exam, I took my felt pens and coloured the map provided in as much detail as I could remember before answering the exam questions.

I totally aced my exam and received an average of 90 per cent. I learnt for the first time that if the 'why' (your passion) is strong enough, the 'how' becomes easy. But my excitement was short-lived. Every airline I applied to told me the same thing: "Insurance does not allow us to employ someone with a visual impairment, not even as ground staff."

For the next year or two, I worked at places related to tourism. Working for the British Consulate and the British Embassy was rewarding. Being part of this outfit during the death of Princess Diana allowed me to see a very sensitive and proud side of the British public. It also gave me great insight into what was then known as the two-year, working holiday visa. While working at the consulate we were placed on rotation. Each month we would move to a different department. This, I thought, was a very well thought-out management strategy as within six months everyone knew the ins and outs of every department and could be used wherever needed at any time.

The work in one of these departments involved dealing with the public – customer service, if you like. Behind a glass panel, people would line up to hand in applications, make payments and receive passports or visas. This proved to be the most difficult department for me to cope with. Payment confirmations and details of customers were printed in small, faded, blue font on a little slip of paper. I had great trouble reading these. Many of the customers got quite upset and irritated with me.

"Can't you see?" an elderly British lady huffed at me. But she wasn't the only one and I eventually asked for a meeting with my manager.

"I'm struggling," I admitted.

"But can't we help? Maybe you can work in the other departments only."

I should have accepted her offer. I learnt, over time, that it was a once-in-a-lifetime offer and that very few such offers would come my way again. I was stubborn and determined, though, and I felt that if I could not succeed in one department, I should not be allowed in any of the departments. And that ultimately, I shouldn't even be there.

I then worked for a company called Travelphone. As part of my job, I assisted in organising conferences. One such event was an international conference for health practitioners and I was tasked with filling goody bags. One product was a large box of breakfast cereal. The shipment arrived late, which meant that we sat stuffing cereal boxes into goody bags throughout the night to have them ready in time for the delegates the next morning. As the key representative at these conferences, I stayed in the same hotel as our delegates and accompanied them from the hotel to the conference venue. They soon learnt that there was no love lost between me and those cereal boxes. The delegates were also given my number and room extension in case of any emergency or general query. This turned out to be my worst nightmare. I received calls at 3am asking me to find spectacles that were left on the coach or at the venue. One lady even called at 2am just to confirm the time the coach would be departing later that morning. I guess this was my experience of the not-so-glamorous side of the travel and tourism industry. On the final day of the conference, the delegates presented me with a gift. Of course, it had to be one of those darn cereal boxes.

We often worked shifts on weekends, and Sundays were especially quiet. One such Sunday I was working with our English-speaking director, Greg. With his blessing, I started doing research into holiday accommodation that was accessible to people with disabilities. I did this by sending enquiries via fax machine to companies in different countries all over the world. A week later, the other director, Hennie, called me in to his office. Hennie was a very large, very bearded man …

"Who said you could waste company money on international faxes?" he yelled at me.

"Greg gave me permission – he even assisted me," I stammered, scared of the big bull of a man who was getting up and making his way towards me.

"Greg is not the boss! I am the boss!" His shouting became louder as he came to stand so close to me that his garlic-loaded breath nearly knocked me out. I was actually quite terrified, when, all of a sudden, out of the blue, my nose began to bleed profusely. I was extremely relieved to have an excuse to rush to the bathroom and get away from this awful bully. After leaving the office that day, I never returned to Travelphone. I wanted to, but my dad intervened and said, "Men like that are not worth your time. I don't want you to work for someone who treats you like that." My dad did not step in often, but when he did, he did it with a strong, protective heart, which I loved, and still do.

During this time of my life I was under the impression that I was part of a very special social circle and that I had made friends for life. Friends who were of the same faith therefore had the same values as mine, or so I thought. The opposite proved to be true. My heart was broken when I was pushed aside for no good reason, yet still today I thank those heartless girls. The hurt they caused pushed me into the best decision I could ever have made. I remember sitting on my bed crying the day it all fell apart. My brother André came in and sat next to me. He had been mistreated and pushed aside by the same people. When I finally looked up at him, I heard him swear for the first time.

"Fuck 'em all sis. Let's move to London!"

Chapter 8: London calling

We did the maths and calculated that, with some hard work, it would take us about three months to save enough money, apply for the working holiday visa and be on our way.

In March 1998, André, Justin and I sat on a Virgin Atlantic plane headed to London. "If this plane goes down," my brother joked, "at least we can say we went down on a virgin." The two boys sat on either side of me and, after our in-flight meal, both fell asleep, each on one of my shoulders. I was too nervous and excited to sleep. With my whole life packed into two rucksacks, I had left South Africa. I had accepted a job as assistant manager at a hotel in Ambleside in the Lake District. A new adventure was about to unfold.

The Horseshoe Inn was owned and run by what initially seemed to be a very agreeable English gentleman. Upon my arrival, I was shown to a room and invited to make myself at home. It was one of the standard single rooms in the hotel and was perfect. I was also presented with a contract, which I signed without really looking at it as my eyes were tired and I didn't want to cause a scene by asking someone else to read it for me.

The next day, I learnt that the position was not for an assistant manager but for a general assistant. This meant doing everything: from taking out the trash and cleaning the pots in the kitchen, to cleaning rooms and waitressing at night. The boss turned out to be miserly beyond anything I had ever experienced. He promptly moved me to a new room on my second day. It was a bunk bed in the laundry room, where the bedding was always damp due to a leaky roof.

Of all my duties, waitressing was the most difficult. Walking from a brightly lit kitchen to a dimly lit dining room meant that I often had very little sight to work with. The guests at the hotel were never happy with the blonde South African waitress taking the wrong orders to the wrong tables. Over the next month, my shifts became longer and longer and the conditions worsened. Come Easter weekend, I asked for one evening off.

"Sir, I've worked for nine days straight on double shifts. Please may I have Sunday evening off to attend a religious event? It is the Lord's Memorial and the most sacred occasion in our faith."

"Don't make your issues mine," he hissed. "It is Easter, no time off for anyone!" I packed my bag and left the old Scrooge with one staff member fewer for the whole of the Easter holiday.

During my short stay at Ambleside, I met a young English girl called Claire. We agreed to rent a room in a house-share in Kendal with two other English girls. I managed to get a job at the Sunlight factory. The company cleaned overalls and workwear from other factories. My first task was to empty the pockets of the overalls from the jam factory before they were washed. I found everything from bottle tops to used condoms and the odd five pence – never anything of real value.

Despite several near misses because of my poor vision, I worked my way up to operating the machine that pressed chefs' jackets. Management had zero regard for health and safety regulations. They had a contact at the department of occupational health and safety who would warn them whenever an inspection was imminent. For the most part, the fire exits were blocked by massive trolleys overflowing with dirty overalls. The workers who raced these trolleys across the factory floor had little regard for whoever was in their way and I was hit on several occasions. I was black and blue but at least I was paid.

At the start of the summer that year, Claire and I decided to move to London. We initially lived with André and Justin, but then moved to a house-share in Beckenham. As long as you weren't too fussy and you were willing to get your hands dirty, there was always work available in London. Though I did not mind any of that, I signed up with a temp agency and tried to get office work instead. I was very excited when the first offer I received was for a receptionist's position at a large corporate in Canary Wharf. Upon arrival, I was given the switchboard extension list for directing incoming calls. It was printed in a very small font so I asked if I might use the photocopier to enlarge it. Although I had informed the agency of my visual impairment, they had not passed the information on to the company where I was placed. I wasn't allowed to enlarge the list and that evening I received a message from the agency asking me not to return the following day. The reason remains a mystery to this day. For the next few weeks, I tried getting answers, but the agent who had placed me refused to take my calls and the agency never offered me another opportunity.

For the next six months, I had too many jobs to mention. My favourite was a six-week temp job at the BBC, Radio Four, transcribing interviews with people who had been close to Frank Sinatra. They were happy with my work and I often thought, "if only my typing teacher from grade nine could see me now."

The other jobs I had during that time were far less glamorous, from doing laundry for an infirmary to a gardening job in an exclusive estate. Probably my worst job during this period was working as an assistant at a sandwich shop and café on the high street in Beckenham. The work was hard and the pay was minimal. This would have been fine had the manageress not been an absolute cow. She was never happy with any of our work. The pharmacist next door was a regular and a friend of hers. One day, he objected profusely when I held his change close to my face before handing it to him. When I tried to explain that I couldn't see very well and had to do so to ensure I'd given him the correct amount, he wasn't satisfied with my answer and complained to Mrs Cow. She very unceremoniously told me I was not to come back to work the following day. When the pharmacist returned later that same day I was still very upset but also quite pleased that I'd have an opportunity to leave my mark …

Pedantic Mr Pharmacist ordered a spud with baked beans and a cup of tea to go. He drove a flashy little sports car with white, leather seats and he always parked in the disabled bay across the road. I prepared his order as usual, but this time with a little something different. I took a needle and made several small holes in the bottom of his polystyrene cup and take-away holder. If all went well, it wouldn't start leaking until he was well on his way in his car. I believe it worked. I never did have the pleasure of witnessing the results of my clever scheme, but imagining the outcome did make me feel a little better.

Though I knew I had been treated unfairly, I had no idea what to do about it. I'll never forget leaving the shop that day. While walking home, my left eye started feeling quite strange and by the evening, I could see nothing from it. By morning it seemed to have cleared up but it never returned to normal. The experience was slightly terrifying and I remember crying myself to sleep that night. Unfortunately, this also marked the beginning of what would be a downward spiral in my vision.

Half-way through my two-year stay in the UK, Claire and I took a break from the bleak English winter and escaped to the African sun – another whirlwind adventure on a shoestring budget. Sandra, our landlady in Beckenham, gave us a bottle of champagne as a parting gift and this travelled with us to Africa. We met our friends from Swaziland in Pretoria and took a long road trip to Mozambique. After an hour or two of chatting away in the car, we naturally became quite thirsty. Although the champagne was warm it seemed the perfect way to start our adventure. We were driving through a small town called Carolina when we decided to open our gift. It was late on a Sunday afternoon and the only place that was open was the petrol station, which we passed as I hung out the window and popped the cork. It broke the silence with quite a bang. The two men working at the petrol station got the fright of their lives. They both fell flat on their stomachs holding their heads not knowing that the shot they heard was not from a gun but from a well-travelled bottle of champagne.

On this trip I learnt that I quite liked skinny-dipping. I also learnt that skinny-dipping as a visually impaired person came with added risks. One evening in Mozambique, Claire and I went for a long stroll along the beach. The tide was low and the beach was dotted with small fishing boats moored in the sand. The moon was nearly full and the water was calm, glistening and inviting. Perfect skinny-dipping conditions. We placed our clothes on one of the little boats and enjoyed the warm water of the Indian Ocean. After a while, Claire emerged from the sea and dressed. I thought she'd probably had enough – poor, inhibited British girl. Once I felt that I'd indulged my temporary lack of inhibition long enough, I, too, left the water. What Claire had failed to mention was that the rest of our travelling party were making their way towards us. Of course, I never saw them. When I finally did, I had nowhere to hide and my clothes were still a hundred yards away. Unfortunately for me, none of them had any kind of visual impairment.

During my stay in London in the late nineties, I dated a guy called Wayne. Wayne was a born and bred Londoner but his parents were from the West Indies. Wayne's skin was the blackest of black and although dating across racial lines was nothing out of the ordinary in London, it was still very controversial in South Africa. I was brought up to be blind to colour and culture and my parents approved of Wayne. Sadly, I could not say the same of everyone else. But just as I was blind towards the colour of his skin, I also couldn't see his true intentions. I was soon replaced by a German pen pal whom he'd never met but then also married at the drop of a hat.

Returning from our African interlude, we again found there were many odd jobs to be done. For a few months, I worked as an assistant at an infirmary where I did the laundry on Sundays. One of my favourite responsibilities was to take tea and biscuits to the residents. All the residents were very particular about how they liked their cuppa. Although I endured some verbal abuse, one elderly, bedridden gentleman approved in no uncertain terms. One morning he took my hand and said, "Darling, will you be mine?" I did not want to upset him and replied: "Maybe tomorrow." I thought by morning the proposal would be long forgotten, but the next morning he greeted me cheerfully: "Darling, is today tomorrow?"

I'd been in the UK for about a year when I started thinking about my Contiki Tours dream again. I learnt that their head office was in Bromley, not far from where I lived at that stage. I took a chance and phoned them to enquire about any vacancies. It happened to be the start of the busy summer season and a temp admin position was available in their operations department. I was interviewed the very next day. During the interview, I explained that I was visually impaired. The manageress, Jo, took one of the tour files and showed it to me asking, "Will this be a problem?"

"Not as long as you don't mind my nose being buried in it." Jo laughed and the job was mine. At the end of summer my role was extended and I worked for Contiki Tours for a year.

The computer system they used was the old black screen kind with yellow or white writing. I managed to work with it by also having my nose stuck to the screen. One day the system was down at the Bromley office and a new staff member based in central London needed help uploading urgent information. I was the only one who was able to talk her through the process.

Seems I had memorised it all over the few months that I had been there. Working at Contiki Tours was a dream come true. Although I was not a tour operator, I was very much part of the process of making travellers' dreams come true.

Chapter 9: Caution: Dangerous driver

When my two-year visa expired I returned to South Africa and Claire joined me. We lived together in Cape Town and spent our time promoting our faith. One winter's afternoon Claire dropped a bombshell on me: "I am planning my future and you are not in it. Make your own plans," she announced. I was gutted. Claire had been my best friend and for neither rhyme nor reason she had cut me from her life completely.

I moved to a small town called Tulbagh, where I worked as a private tutor for three German children. During this time I met Desiré and Monique, two sisters from Worcester, a town nearby. They turned out to be friends for life and together we would embark on a journey with incredible highs and lows. Whatever troubles we had to face or accomplishments we would celebrate, we would never do it alone. Also during this time, though, one of my greatest challenges started rearing its ugly head: losing what I had left of my sight.

When I was a child, my parents and I were told that although my sight was not great, it would not deteriorate. Experiencing the symptoms of various eye diseases for the first time was a horrible shock. Solid black spots appearing and disappearing at regular intervals were a sign of macular degeneration. Losing peripheral vision was a symptom of retinitis pigmentosa. As it turned out, I had none of these conditions. The reason I was experiencing a wide variety of symptoms was because the eye had never fully developed and was now showing signs of degeneration. This is possible when one has ROP (retinopathy of prematurity). The extent to which this degenerative condition affects one's sight depends on when you were born and what treatment was available at the time.

By that time, I had moved to Worcester to be closer to Desiré and Monique. Worcester is well known for the school for the blind based there and for several other organisations supporting people with disabilities. It was the perfect place to be as the residents were very disability aware. I assumed this would make finding a job quite easy. I was wrong.

I remember having to do a typing test with several other applicants as part of the interview process for a job at a large corporate. We took the test at a local college. Oh no! Déjà vu, I was back in grade nine! I asked if I could use a stand or just a stack of books to bring the test paper closer to my face. I was told that would be unfair to all the other applicants and that everyone else would have to do the same. I was furious. Needless to say, my request for extra time also was not granted. The test was a pure typing speed test. When the time was up, each applicant's typed pages were printed. Everyone had two pages except me. The moderator looked up and asked, "Where is your second page?"

"Probably devoured by your lack of disability awareness," I replied.

It goes without saying that I did not get the job.

After six months of relentless job hunting and too many unsuccessful interviews to mention, I finally got a break. DeafBlind South Africa was looking for a development coordinator. This time, my sight was not a factor and I aced the interview. It was also the starting block to my career in the charity sector. Although I was employed as a development coordinator, it soon became clear that the organisation needed to focus on fundraising as their financial situation was not great. On a prior trip to the UK, I visited DeafBlind UK and saw them host a fundraiser called Jailbreak. Willing supporters of an organisation would agree to be 'arrested' and would then have to raise 'bail money' to secure their release. After three months of nagging, the National Director of DeafBlind SA agreed that I could do a Jailbreak in South Africa. It was a huge success. Organising the event cost less than R1 000, while we raised just over R50 000. This was the first of many more jailbreaks to come. The concept was not new but we added real value for participants by using real policemen and women and real police vans for the arrest and transport of our 'criminals'. We also took mug shots, and fingerprints with the old-fashioned, black ink method. The photos and prints, and a DVD of their arrests, were given to the participants as a souvenir. The following year many of them became 'repeat offenders'.

The director of DeafBlind SA and I did not always see eye to eye, especially about the management of funds. When I was offered the role of fundraising and marketing manager with the Association for the Sensory Disabled (ASD), I grabbed it with both hands. We hosted several jailbreaks across the Western Cape every year and, by doing so, gained long-term donors for the small organisation. ASD is still operating and doing great work for children with multi-sensory and other disabilities. The organisation still hosts very profitable annual jailbreaks. They also established a day-care centre for multi-sensory, disabled children – the first of its kind in the country. It is still going strong today, making a huge difference in the lives of these kids and their families.

Although I was reminded of my deteriorating eyesight daily, I simply would not accept what was happening. At first, a very stubborn me lived in absolute denial and would not acknowledge at all what was happening. My greatest fear was losing my independence. As a result, I made decisions that took stubbornness to a whole new level. Some might even call it severe stupidity…

Desiré had bought a second-hand road bike – a 250cc Kawasaki. I desperately wanted to ride it and categorically insisted on being in the saddle. It was a Sunday morning when Des finally relented and showed me the ropes. My first ride was a very slow, careful and calculated drive around the block. I had immense respect for the motorbike and was very well aware of the pain and injury that could result from falling on a tar road. Later that afternoon, we took the bike to a deserted airfield. This is where stupidity took over and I threw caution to the wind. Des agreed that I could drive, with her as a passenger on the back. I was immediately transported to my childhood days and imagined being back on my bicycle, racing the imaginary dirt racetrack between my school and our home. The only thing I concentrated on was opening the throttle. Everything happened in slow motion after that. Des could see the pending disaster unfolding and managed to jump off the bike just before I lost control and crashed. I skidded down the dirt track with the motorbike on top of me. When I came to I was lying flat on the ground with Des and Monique worriedly hovering above me. The pain was excruciating. But it was a Sunday afternoon. And I did not have medical aid. Monique took the bike home, while Des lifted me into her car and drove to the nearest shop so we could stock up on cheap painkillers and Coke.

Later that week, Des came to my flat to see how I was doing. The previous few days had been a very rough combination of pain, episodes of fainting and being sick. For some reason, we thought it would be a good idea to go down to the local pub for a beer and a game of pool. At our local, the Peter Potter, I slowly made my way up the stairs with my crutches. I had enough money for only one beer so this would be a short visit. A large, elderly man approached Des and me. We called him Uncle Elephant. He was a big but gentle soul and, as it turned out, used to be the mayor of the town. We started chatting about travel and tourism in the local area, something we were both passionate about. He offered us some red wine and would not take no for an answer. The wine was disgusting but Uncle Elephant didn't seem to think so. Every time we'd turn our heads, our glasses would be refilled. We were both taught that it was rude not to accept hospitality shown. And so we drank. And drank.

Just after 11pm we finally managed to make our excuses. I felt fantastic. I had no more pain and can remember dancing down the pub stairs, never mind walking. I did so without my crutches, which I actually forgot at the pub. Fortunately I lived close by and as we neared my flat, I told Des I wanted to stay outside for a while. I went and sat in the middle of the warm tar road. I loved it and stayed there for some time. When I finally went into my flat, Des was passed out on the floor, snoring away. I thought of doing the same but was stopped in my tracks and suddenly felt very ill. There was no way I could make it to the bathroom and I threw up in the kitchen sink. First it was copious amounts of vile red wine, followed by awful, bitter dregs that tasted of cheap painkillers. I had been living on these for days. I finally slumped into bed at about 4am.

When I woke up, EVERYTHING hurt. My headache was the least of my worries. My dancing escapades down the pub stairs had exacerbated the injury to my knee. Des phoned my employer and explained that I had terrible flu and could not come in that day. I did the same for her. After three coffees Des put her foot down. "I am taking you to the public hospital, no arguing."

I spent the next year on crutches nursing a badly injured knee and an equally bruised ego.

It stands to reason that I would have learnt my lesson from that experience but only a few months later, I was presented with the opportunity to be in the driving seat again and took it with zero hesitation. I was not going to miss out.

Francois lived and worked on a wine farm just outside Worcester. He'd had the hots for Desiré for many years and would do just about anything to impress this elusive girl. He was in the process of revamping an old, red Volkswagen Beetle. It looked so inviting with no roof and the red paint gleaming in the afternoon sun. When I asked Francois if I could take the car for a spin on the farm road, he said yes without hesitation because he was sure this would get him into Desiré's good books.

The drive was brilliant but the dirty windshield made it impossible to see as I was driving straight into the setting afternoon sun. I heard voices yelling at me to turn but my reactions were too slow and my foot seemed to be stuck to the accelerator. With a huge crash, I drove straight into a thick vineyard pole. There were no serious injuries but I had to pay for a new windscreen, which caused serious hurt to my budget.

That evening, Des made me promise her that I'd hang up my driving gloves for good. I guess she made some sense – my failing eyesight was finally catching up with me.

While living in Worcester, I was introduced to blind navigators' rallies. Do not fear – 'blindies' don't do the driving, we only navigate. We'd receive a set of instructions and then have to communicate these to our driver. Along the route there were checkpoints that we had to reach within a certain timeframe. The aim was to be as close as possible to the set time. Every second that you arrived either too soon or too late, would count against you. The team with the least points at the end of the journey won.

My first rally was at a venue just outside of Cape Town. My driver was very calm and explained everything to me perfectly. We worked so well together that we actually won. I was totally surprised. There were a few disgruntled folks who said that our victory was unfair because I was not completely blind. But each visual impairment holds its own challenges. Braille readers, for example, would not be affected by direct sunlight and bumps in the road. I did not let them ruin our win.

At the next rally, Desiré was my driver. It seemed like a great idea at the time but thanks to my wobbly, jumpy eyes, without knowing it, I skipped two instructions. "At the next crossing, go straight," I read out loud to Desiré.

"We can't," she said.

"We have to, that is what it says here!" I said, slightly annoyed.

"We are at a T-junction."

"Oh dear."

We missed a checkpoint, which came with a huge time penalty. We were lucky not to get the wooden spoon that day.

Chapter 10: A love lost

Not long after I moved to Worcester, Des introduced me to her friend Drew. He was a one-in-a-million guy. He became part of our group and we were inseparable. We went on road trips and weekends away. Being the only lad amongst three ladies, Drew was positively beaming, but his heart longed for only one, Desiré. Free-spirited though she was, it would take a lot of graft from Drew to win her over. I became his wingman, so to speak, and it resulted in a close friendship. There were moments when I thought that my feelings for him might be more than just friendship, but I cared enough to know who made him happy: Desiré.

In 2002, the four of us spent New Year's Eve together in Jeffrey's Bay. On New Year's Day, we celebrated the New Year with a bang by doing a bungee jump from the Gouritz River Bridge – the world's highest bungee jump above dry ground.

Our next trip was not far off. We were planning a road trip to Pretoria to surprise Claire, who was in the country for a visit. We all met at Desiré and Monique's home, where Drew would pick us up for the carefully planned, 12-hour drive. Drew was late. He was never late. When we called him, his phone went straight to voicemail. This was also very unlike him. Outside it was raining and a thunderstorm raged over the

Breede River Valley with ominous ferocity. Drew drove a black Golf TDI 4 so his car was easily recognisable. One of Desiré's colleagues called to say that there had been an accident in the Du Toit's Kloof Pass and that the vehicle looked like Drew's car. The three of us jumped into Desiré's car and rushed to the crash site. I was sitting in the backseat calling Drew's phone over and over again. Only a voicemail replied to my hopes and prayers. When we reached the accident scene, our worst fears were realised. It was Drew's car and it was lying on its roof with Drew still inside. The fact that Des had driven with such great speed, meant that we had arrived there before the ambulance.

It was raining even harder now and the thunder and lightning kept drowning out commands shouted by bystanders on the scene. The rain made it even more difficult for me to see so I got out of the car and stood on the side of the road. I would only have been in the way if I'd gone any closer. Drew was not conscious but he was still alive. He had a severe head injury. Des and Monique drove off to meet the ambulance at the hospital. It was decided that I would go in the ambulance but when I tried to get in, the paramedic simply refused to allow it. I stood there alone on the mountain pass, tears and rain streaming down my face.

A young man driving a tow truck came to my rescue. He spotted me and offered me a lift to the hospital. Once at the hospital, I kept on thinking that I needed to pray, and desperately so, but no matter how hard I tried, I simply couldn't. Drew's family and friends arrived soon after. There were so many people and yet I had never felt so alone in all my life. They allowed Desiré to go through to see Drew. Sometime later she came walking down the hallway towards me. Before I had a chance to ask, she threw her arms around me. In a voice filled with pain and shock she said, “His heart could not cope with the injuries. He didn’t make it.”

As we started making our way home from the hospital, I phoned my parents to let them know about Drew. Having to speak those words, “Drew is dead,” broke something inside of me. Just as the tears wanted to come I pushed the emotion back. Who was I to cry? I was not his partner. I was not his family. I had held no place in his life. I was not at liberty to grieve. This unhelpful pattern of thinking lasted well over six months and eventually resulted in a nervous breakdown. Post-traumatic stress is what they called it. It took many long hours of therapy for me to finally admit that I did love him, that he was an amazing friend and that I had every right to grieve.

Because Worcester had so many visually-impaired residents, in a way, it felt like being back at Prinshof. I wasn’t all that different from almost everyone else and this gave me a bit more confidence socially. Being romantically pursued was something very new to me. It was one of the few times in my life when my deteriorating eyesight was not an issue. But because I was not dealing with the emotional trauma associated with losing one’s sight or the trauma of losing Drew, I became excessively reckless in areas where I still had some confidence left. This led to several brief relationships with young men who were all blind. I believe I hurt several people in the process because, as soon as it became serious, I got out. At the time, I believed that I started feeling trapped whenever a relationship became serious simply because I had not met the right man. The real reason would reveal itself years later.

Chapter 11: A four-legged miracle

I'll never forget the day a friend suggested I apply for a guide dog. "Guide dogs are only for people with complete loss of sight, I'd never qualify," I replied. My friend did her homework though and convinced me to investigate the matter further. She was right; I would qualify. In hindsight, I realise that applying for a guide dog became the first step in a lifelong process of learning to accept my loss of sight.

The application process was quite lengthy and involved. I'd not had any white-cane or mobility training before and this was a prerequisite for applying. Me? With a white cane? Please! After many pleas and long heart-to-hearts with my friends, I agreed to go for white-cane training in Cape Town. I did it but I hated it. It made me feel awkward and ugly. A white cane certainly wasn't a fashion accessory and to me it felt like it was screaming to the world: "I am broken!"

Two years after starting the process, I was finally invited to Johannesburg to attend training for a guide dog. Those three weeks were both the best and the worst of my life. My elder brother Hannes had just passed away at the tender age of 30. I did what I do best: I buried my head in the sand and just prayed that the hurt would go away. In contrast to this hurt and sadness, doing the guide-dog training was an amazing experience. Sandy, a yellow Labrador, was introduced to me and we made the perfect team. At the start of my training I was still scared that I'd fail because I could still see a little and, once I got to know a place, I could get along very well by myself. The true revelation came when we did our first night walk. I had no choice but to put my trust 100 per cent in Sandy. She was my very own four-legged miracle.

Calling a guide dog a miracle is not an exaggeration. When you see a guide dog and its owner walking down the street, there is so much more going on than just a dog guiding a blind person around potentially harmful obstacles. On the practical side of things, a guide dog is more intelligent and helpful than some humans I know. Yes, she does guide me around harmful obstacles. With a white cane, I first had to touch those obstacles and then navigate my way around them. When you're being assisted by a guide dog, you're not aware of most obstacles as your guide dog leads you obliviously around them.

Loss of peripheral vision is often compared to tunnel vision. This means that obstacles near your sides and your head, like overhanging branches, become a problem. Guide dogs are trained to take these into consideration as well. Those branches can do more than cause a bad hair day – bumping into them can result in serious injury.

A guide dog is a miracle like no other, emotionally and psychologically. Its companionship and unconditional love take the place of loneliness and despair. For me, the greatest miracle of a guide dog was how much of my independence and self-confidence I regained. Like many disabilities, a visual impairment deprives you of these things. Continually having to ask for help eats away at your self-esteem. The result is that you stop asking and you stop living. Your home becomes your prison and you become a mere spectator of life. With a guide dog, you become more mobile. Very seldom do you have to ask for help. You get up, you go out and you enjoy life with your pride intact.

My life started to transform and soon Worcester felt too small for me. A move to Cape Town was on the cards. Was I ready for a job change? Experience had proven this process to be soul-destroying. This time, however, things were different. I had become us. Sandy and I were a team and together we could move mountains. I applied for a fundraising position at the Community Chest in Cape Town. At the final interview, Sandy and I turned on the charm and won the hearts of the interview panel.

By that time Monique and Desiré were also based in Cape Town and the four of us shared a house in Durbanville. Every morning at 5:30, Sandy and I would take the bus to Cape Town and walk the six long blocks to our new office in the centre of town. The jailbreak concept was a hit with the Community Chest management team. We held several jailbreaks, my favourite of which were the West Coast events. Sandy became a bit of a celebrity and happily posed for as many photos as she needed to.

Cape Town was fun but it was also dangerous. Sandy and I were a soft target in the city centre and I was robbed of my phone on several occasions. Even in the small town of Worcester we'd become a target. I remember one hot midweek afternoon walking down the busy high street. Suddenly, a man stood in front of me. When I went left, so did he. Went I went right, he followed.

“Idiot!” I thought, and told Sandy to “Up up, quickly girl!” She found her way around the idiot and that was that. Or so we thought. About three blocks later, a young man came running towards us.

“Madam, madam!” he called out of breath. “Did you know that man had a knife?” I had no idea.

“And he stole your phone,” he stammered, still out of breath. “But don’t worry madam, we chased him and beat the shit out of him. Here is your phone.”

I was shocked but relieved and so grateful that these men had stepped in and helped me. What was a very great concern is that I had not even seen the knife in the mugger’s hand.

Having Sandy at my side reminded me that anything was possible as long as I gave it my all. My dream was to return to London. Desiré had already relocated to London in 2004 and Monique wanted to join her. I encouraged them to travel but I did not want to miss out. After doing extensive research, I learnt that studying in the UK would be my best option. “Project London” was set into motion. For both Sandy and me to be able to go, I’d need to source a lot of funding. I sold everything I owned and, again with only a rucksack, I was on my way. This time though, I was not alone. Sandy was coming, too.

Chapter 12: Discrimination in London

We left in May 2005. Sandy had to fly in the hold of the aircraft, along with all the other pets, and had to go into quarantine for six months. Looking back, I'd never do that again. Thankfully, I'd also never have to, as those regulations have long since changed. It was incredibly tough on both of us. We did, however, pull through and by December, the two blonde girls were back together, ready for life and all its opportunities.

For the first few months, I managed to rent a room from one of my previous landladies. Sadly, she wasn't keen on "having a dog in the house", and I had to look for alternative accommodation. It seemed simple at first but became a nightmare that lasted for several years.

Being on a student visa, I was allowed to work for only 20 hours a week and only on a low-level salary. This, and the fact that I had to pay for my studies, left me with very little money. All I could afford was a room in a house-share. Housemates come in different shapes, sizes and levels of intelligence and hygiene. I had a certain knack for picking the worst of them. At first everything would seem fine and well. Then, just as soon as I felt I had settled, the nastiness would appear. Having a guide dog also closed many doors for me on the housing front.

When I first realised that I would simply have to get a place of my own, I was quite excited. After some research, I found that there were places set up specifically for the visually impaired. One of the organisations that provided such accommodation was Action for Blind People. At the time, the only place they had available was in Epsom – a two-hour journey from work. On the day I went to meet the staff, I explained that I was on a student visa and did not have a British passport. They said it would not be a problem and I moved in the following Sunday. The bachelor's flat was great but had no appliances, so I used what little savings I had left to buy a microwave and a small refrigerator. The staff member on duty that day made a copy of my passport and everything seemed fine. A few days later, however, I was informed that I was not entitled to any benefits. Not only had I known this but I had told the manager that I'd made this very clear when I first met with her team. She then explained that I'd have to pay a much higher rental. I was stunned.

"I don't even earn that amount each month," I explained.

'Well then you need to leave," she said.

"But I have nowhere to go," I exclaimed.

"That is not my problem."

I was given until the end of the week to vacate the flat.

I searched high and low for a room to rent. As soon as a landlord heard that Sandy would be joining me, I would get a definitive no, and have the phone smacked down in my ear. I had only one day left. I was sitting on the train in tears when finally something came through. There was a room available in a multi-share house in Mill Hill East in North London. The house had three bedrooms and there would be nine people sharing one bathroom. My room had a door to the outside garden, which made it more expensive, but perfect for Sandy.

The agent must have seen me coming a mile away: a blind girl in desperate need of a place to stay. I had to put down a cash deposit that same evening. The room had several other attributes that I came to discover over the next few days. No insulated flooring, just carpet on concrete. No proper ceiling, which afforded me a live performance, with incredible sound that shook the walls, by the doped-up DJ on the floor above. Worst of all, there was no heating. Because the Christmas holidays were approaching, the agent said this could be attended to only in the New Year. It was absolutely freezing. Breaking all guide-dog training rules, Sandy and I shared a bed every night just to keep warm. I had to find something else.

During my online search for a room to rent, I came across a company called Spacelet. They served as an agent and specialised in rooms to rent in house shares. They had a wide variety of places on their books, especially in the areas I was interested in. I called and they explained that I had to pay an admin fee before I could see any rooms on their books. It was around 50 pounds, which was steep, but I understood they had to make money, too. I informed them of my situation.

The lady I spoke to happened to be the owner, Mrs Gomez.

"Ma'am I am looking for a double room. I am visually impaired and I have a guide dog, Sandy," I explained.

"That's fine but we charge double for any customers with pets."

"Sandy is not a pet ma'am, she is a guide dog. She is a highly-trained, qualified guide dog."

"That does not change anything. The same policy would apply."

"Ma'am, I believe that is against the law and would be seen as discrimination. I can report you to the DRC."

"What is the DRC?"

"The Disability Rights Commission."

"Well, you just go ahead and do that!" she said, slamming the phone down.

And that was the end of that.

I managed to find a housing solution, but again it was short-lived and I soon found myself looking for alternative accommodation. Again, every advert I found directed me to Spacelet. This time I did my enquiries in writing via email and received the same response. I was told in writing that it did not matter that Sandy was a guide dog; I still had to pay double. I was heartbroken and frustrated but this time round I did not take it lying down. I reported Mrs Gomez.

At first, the legal proceedings went as planned. My representative, Joan, from North London, did a great job. Unfortunately, she relocated and I was given a new representative, Miss Moon. We met at London Bridge station, where I updated her on my case. We were very close to getting a result. She assured me of her support and she seemed sincere. She said she'd contact all the relevant parties, including Mrs Gomez.

When I had not heard from her for some time, I called to hear what progress she had made. This was the start of two years of emails and phone calls into the abyss. She never made any progress and always had some excuse to put me off. In the meantime, I was still contributing to Legal Aid every month. I nearly gave up hope, but instead decided to email her superior. Absolutely all hell broke loose. The date to submit my case had long passed and this meant there was no chance of receiving any recompense. I was furious, but so was Miss Moon's superior. He launched his own investigation and in the end I did receive some monetary compensation.

I was never told exactly why, but Miss Moon was struck off the roll for malpractice shortly afterwards. I can only imagine that she and Mrs Gomez had struck some kind of underhanded deal.

Chapter 13: Home sweet home

Sandy wasn't the only reason accommodation was hard to find. My lack of sight was a huge problem for some landlords. One East London landlord insisted on a letter from the local council indemnifying him against any risk should I injure myself living on his property. Only by the time I had Rikki, my second guide dog, did I manage to find a landlady who was not blinded by my disability. Living in Brunel Road was like hitting the jackpot. It was a lovely area, my housemates were reasonable and it was close to work.

When I called the landlord, I made no mention of Rikki and decided I'd introduce her at our first meeting instead. Rikki charmed her way into my landlady's heart and the strategy worked. Our stay in Brunel Road was an amazing time but was cut short way too soon. The landlady was selling and we were asked to move to the house her husband owned, just across the road.

This is where I met the Cave family. Paul, his wife Kerry and daughter were South Africans, popularly known as Saffas, too. They informed me that our landlord was not nearly as agreeable as his wife. The washing machine had been broken for ages and the mattresses were in a very poor state. I had a moment of brilliance and, with Paul's help, we swapped the mattresses and washing machine with those in his wife's house on the day I moved. Sharing a home with the Cave family was very exciting as they were expecting a new baby. Though I'd never really felt very maternal, or that I had a biological clock that was ticking away, there was something truly special about a new little human entering this world. Jodi was his parents' absolute pride and joy.

Late one evening I was watching telly while waiting for my turn in the bathroom. The porn-industry equivalent of the Oscars came on and, to my utter disbelief, the short man who lived next door appeared on the screen. He had been nominated in the best male actor category.

"Paul! Kerry! Come quickly!" I shouted. I needed to know if my eyes were deceiving me, but for once they were not. The programme showed clips from the neighbour's movies and he bloody well won everything. In one clip, wearing, to our amazement, a Springbok rugby jersey, he stood eating a sandwich after an action scene. It suddenly all made sense – the expensive sports car, the Ducati motorbike and the odd working hours. Everyone stood in shock except for me. I was already thinking of ideas on how to approach our neighbour to sponsor a fundraising project.

A few months after Jodi's birth, the house we lived in was put up for sale as well and we were all back to square one. With my colleagues' assistance, I managed to find a small, single room in a house-share with a nurse, a Pilates teacher and a self-employed bloke. It wasn't Brunel Road, but it was good enough for us. The housemates seemed fine, at least initially ... Sharing a house with a male is never easy but this bloke turned out to be the personification of housemate from hell.

My room was next to the toilet and bathroom. The toilet door always stuck a little and needed a good whack or kick to open or close. This meant that I always knew when someone was in there and for how long. Steve often spent quite some time on the throne to take a dump, and then when he left, he would dash down the stairs to the kitchen, bypassing the bathroom and any chance of cleaning his grubby paws. He stepped up a notch in the realm of hideous housemates by stealing some of my luxuries like cheese and bubble-bath.

Steve had an affair with Julie, the nurse living in the room downstairs. He made her keep it a secret even when she fell pregnant. The landlord and Steve were always busy with some sort of deal, which in time would turn sour. The bailiffs came knocking one day when I was the only one at the house. They asked me to tell the landlord that they would be back soon. This culminated in us all having to look for a new place to stay. The Pilates teacher, Anna, invited me to share a house with her and her friend Nancy, who was a personal trainer. It sounded like heaven – a house with no horny, grubby, thieving men.

We moved into a house in Woodford Green. My room was very small with no wardrobes. I had to keep all my clothes in the garage downstairs. The girls promised me that this would change. Meanwhile they lived in luxury, each of them in her own large room upstairs. For some reason, they slept in the same room most nights, yet only Nancy was gay. Anna insisted that she was not and became very upset if I even so much as hinted that she was.

The promise of renovations and a better space for Rikki and me never materialised, yet I had to pay the same rent as everyone else. The stress in the house became unbearable as Nancy turned out to be a passive-aggressive bully. One summer weekend, the two girls went on a break to the coast and I had the house to myself. Gin and tonics and my hubbly were the order of the day. After enjoying a few G&Ts outside, I thought it time to move the party-for-one indoors. As luck would have it, a piece of burning charcoal from the pipe fell onto the living room carpet and quickly burnt a very visible black hole. I panicked. The Shisha pipe had to go outside immediately. I picked it up and rushed down the stairs, dropping tiny embers along the way. The black burn hole now had little companions all along the carpeted stairs.

I was more than willing to accept responsibility for the damage and had sourced several quotes to fix the damage before the girls' return in two days' time. But the carpet was old and it turned out to be impossible to find the same type and colour. Then again, replacing the carpet had been one of the items at the top of the promised redecorating list when we moved in.

When the girls arrived home, I explained my mistake and my wish to put things right. I thought Nancy was going to explode. I eventually went to hide in my room. I was convinced that this would be the night Nancy actually physically attacked me. The next day, I was informed that the only way I would be able to repair the situation was to replace the carpets throughout the house at my own cost. "This is not fair," I thought. But no matter how hard I tried, Nancy, especially, would not listen to reason. Every time the subject was broached, she would react more and more aggressively.

After lots of advice and input from friends and colleagues, I used the opportunity during their next breakaway to move out. Within two days, I had moved, changed my number, and cut all ties that would link me to them. Fortunately, they had insisted that I not be included in the rental contract, so I had no legal obligation towards anyone and this made my great escape a little easier.

It was the summer of 2011 when, having lived in London for just over six years, I realised my elusive dream of finding a safe, comfortable nest for my four-legged partner and me. We moved into a small bachelor's flat in the Pocklington Lodge in West London near Hammersmith. The Pocklington Trust, like Action for Blind People, provided accommodation that was specifically adapted for independent, visually-impaired adults. Flat 19 was small but it was ours. I had to pinch myself every time I entered my flat – just to make sure it was real. Quite appropriately, Roxette had just release a new single: ' She's got nothing on, but the radio'. I'd often celebrate by dancing about with nothing on but the radio.

The Lodge had so many great features. Guide dogs were welcomed and a spending pen (where they did their business) was made available to them. There were many four-legged miracles living in this building. There was a communal laundry facility, with both washing machines and dryers. It also had an administrative office that was available to us during office hours. We could approach them, for example, to decipher our mail, or to help with maintenance around our flats. Best of all, there were two pubs only a stumbling distance away. I was also sure that sharing an entire building with a bunch of blindies would be interesting.

Health and safety is of utmost importance in the UK and the standards and precautions taken at Pocklington Lodge were a shining example of this. Fire alarms were very sensitive.

Should the fire alarm in any of the 40 flats be set off, the whole building would be evacuated. There is always chaos when any building is evacuated but when it's a bunch of blindies, oh my! Only once the fire brigade had assessed the situation and given us a health and safety lecture, would we be allowed back into our warm flats. During this lecture, the number of the flat where the alarm was set off would be revealed. Woe to you if this happened to be your flat.

My first experience of this rather cumbersome procedure was when Blind Blabbermouth Barbara burnt toast at 3am in the middle of winter.

"Who makes toast at 3am?" I hissed as I realised that I had forgotten my shoes in my rush to evacuate.

I turned to a fellow frozen evacuee and said, very confidently, "If Blabbermouth Barb spent half as much time improving her cooking skills as she did gossiping, we would not be standing here. I am no master chef, but this would never happen to me."

Cooking definitely was not one of my many talents, but after numerous flops and failures, I had eventually mastered my signature dish: popcorn. I can make the most perfect batch of popcorn you'll ever taste. And I'm so confident in my own skill, I can do it with my eyes closed.

One unusually warm and sunny Saturday afternoon I was preparing the most perfectly popped batch of popcorn known to all of mankind. I had half on ear on the telly and half an ear on the popcorn when I realised there was a soccer match on TV. This would explain the buzz among my neighbours. England was playing Italy and, for once, England wasn't faring too badly. At the start of the second half, the scores were tied: Italy 1, England 1. I was hooked. I was standing in front of the telly, drink in hand, cheering on the Poms when I heard that most god-awful sound: Beep, beep, beep, the alarm screamed. Whoever was responsible could not have chosen a worse time. Blithering blind idiots! I thought. And then I became aware of it – the tell-tale smell of burnt popcorn …

We were eventually allowed back inside just in time to hear the final whistle – England 2, Italy 1. It would take a while for me to live this one down.

But karma was not quite done with me. It was a typical, cold, rainy Monday morning in March. I found it almost impossible to get out of bed and was virtually being held hostage by my duvet. When I finally managed to escape, I stumbled to the kitchen, popped my cereal in the microwave and dashed towards the safety of a warm shower ... Ahhh, lovely!

Beep, beep, beep, beep!

I stumbled out of the shower as fast as I could. I was dripping wet but there wasn't much time so all I managed to grab was my robe and my cane. Thank goodness my neighbours couldn't see.

Big, blind Barry was leaning on his cane when he muttered, "So who's the blind nutter this time?" No takers. The fireman appeared. "Who is in number 19? Flat 19?"

“That’s me but ... how?” I stammered. He presented me with my cereal bowl, burnt to a crisp. In my drowsy state, I had set the microwave to one hour instead of one minute, and I had forgotten the milk. My friends at the lodge eventually forgave me. One very kind neighbour even suggested an online cookbook: www.mrdelivery.com.

Chapter 14: Any job would do

The challenge of finding suitable accommodation in London pales in comparison with that of finding suitable employment. As with Contiki Tours, I already had my dream job in mind. I wanted to work for Guide Dogs UK. I wanted to be part of the organisation that had changed my life and the lives of so many other blind people. I wanted to join their fundraising team and I was sure my passion would ensure my success.

Well before departing to London I had started investigating the possibility of working for Guide Dogs. Unfortunately, now that I was finally here, they had no vacancies and my dream had to be shelved for the time being. I was, however, determined to work in the charity sector, which would tie in with the experience I gained in South Africa. I was very meticulous in recording each and every job I had applied for. It was a six-month long struggle. I found the entire process quite draining and every unsuccessful application chipped away at my confidence.

All in all, I had applied for 78 jobs during this time. I received 52 replies of which 41 were positive. Of the 41 positives, I made it through to 28 final interviews. Each and every one of the 28 final interviews was unsuccessful. When I had enquired why, not one prospective employer would supply me with a reason.

By law, they were not allowed to refuse me because of my disability, but that did not stop them from doing so. As long as it was not recorded, there would be no legal ramifications for them. At most of the organisations, the interview process itself was not very accessible to me. I was caught between a rock and a hard place. Had I informed them in advance of my needs as a visually-impaired candidate, they could deny me even an interview invitation. And should I not inform them, I placed myself in the very precarious position of having to navigate numerous barriers when taking tests and completing tasks as part of the interview process.

I recall one application in particular. It was with Sense UK, the charity for children with multi-sensory disabilities. I was very excited about this application. I knew the organisation and respected them for the work they did. I had also done volunteer work for them in the past, so I was no stranger to them. While completing the application, I was not shy about my needs and when the day of the interview arrived, I was excited and confident.

Upon arrival, I was asked to do a written task on a computer as part of the interview. I asked if I was allowed to enlarge the fonts on the screen and if the curtains could be closed to reduce the glare on the screen. My requests were denied. During the oral interview, I communicated my disappointment with the situation. I was told the test did not really matter but I believe the damage was done. Again, I was unsuccessful and again, I was never told why.

While this process continued, life did not stand still and bills had to be paid. I had no choice but to take any job I could find. It was during this time that London saw the Battle of Britain's free newspapers. One of these was *The London Paper.* I got a job handing these out to commuters – 3 000 within three hours to be exact. Me being me, there were no half measures and I made it my mission to do my job well. I was loud and I was friendly. Standing with my cane in the busy streets of London, I became quite good at what I did. A Kiwi working for the opposing paper across the street was not happy. The better I got, the worse he did. When I turned my back, he would tip over my trolley, papers flying everywhere. When that did not work, he called the police. I have no idea what lies he told them, but whatever it was, it worked, because I was asked to move to a different location. The officer had zero interest in listening to anything I had to say. My team leader also refused to assist me. Apparently she was too far away. A whole three blocks away. But my next spot worked just as well, until a man selling *The Big Issue* started harassing me. *The London Paper* management was never interested in supporting me. After three gruelling months of handing out thousands of papers and being covered in newspaper ink daily, I called it a day.

During that summer, I got a temp call-centre job with the charity group, Comic Relief. It was only a few weeks of work but I loved it. That year they did the Comic Relief Mile and I was tasked to sign up people who phoned in. I also volunteered at the event itself. I had to escort lesser-known celebrities from the finish line back to the hotel where the reception was held. Sandy was still in quarantine so I had only my cane – which came in very handy when warding off unwanted attention from excited and overzealous fans. That same year, I managed to get another temp position at a small charity called Rhett Syndrome UK. I was able to assist in their office and at some of their events. This helped to repair some of the damage my confidence had suffered during the months of unsuccessful job applications.

It had been six very arduous months since I had arrived in London. I decided it was time to dust off my dream of working for Guide Dogs, and put it back into action. I hoped that if I volunteered for them in my spare time, I would be able to prove myself. I called and was invited to go into their Woodford office for an informal chat to see what volunteering opportunities might be available. I remember feeling ill that day and I almost cancelled but, fortunately, decided to push through.

Upon arrival, I met Nick and Devina, who were on the fundraising team. We had a lovely chat over tea and biscuits. I told them about the work I had done in South Africa, in particular the success I had enjoyed with Jailbreak. When we came to the end of our discussion, Nick asked me to wait in the reception area while he and Devina discussed a few things. When they called me back in, Nick offered me a job – not a volunteering role, no, a paid job within the community fundraising team. I remember standing at Woodford station after they dropped me off. I had kept my poise quite well until then. The minute they left, I let go. I was yelling and singing and dancing on the platform until my train home arrived. Another dream come true.

Chapter 15: A brilliant blind student?

Studying was one way to obtain a visa to live in London and it had always been a dream of mine to further my education. Before I left for London, I applied to Fulham and Chelsea College, a small institution in South West London. The college was happy to accept my application. I started my studies in July of 2005 and embarked upon gaining a degree in business management. The first year was fine until I experienced difficulties with accessing material for quantitative methods. The college directed me to ABE (Association for Business Executives), the examining body. I explained my concerns to them, upon which they supplied the formulas in what they thought would be an accessible format. They simply enlarged the A4 page to A3 and increased the font size to 16. This was not adequate and I still couldn't read it. I needed it in an electronic format that was accessible. The representative of ABE was not impressed that his first attempt was not sufficient. I remember reading his reply in complete and utter disbelief:

"For you to be unable to distinguish between these characters at this size font, leads me to think that it is not just a visual impairment that you have – there may be a sorting gene at fault that no amount of printed modification is going to address."

After months of me fighting my case, ABE allowed me to do a quantities methods project for my final mark and not sit the actual exam. It was not ideal, but it allowed me to find the material myself and complete the project. My goal was to pass quantitative methods, not to become an activist for disability rights. Looking back, I realise I should have obtained legal advice on the matter.

During my second exam, I became ill and was not able to write the paper in one subject. I had a doctor's certificate and the head of the college told me that everything was in order. The next day, though, he called me in to his office. He closed the door and informed me that I had to sit the exam the following day. I explained to him that I could not prepare for the exam because I was ill and therefore could not do it the next day. He was a big, bullish bloke from New Zealand. My refusal to follow his instructions did not go down well. He started shouting at me, threatening that he would have me deported. I was so scared that the only thing I could do was to stand up and walk out, but that only made him even more furious. As I was running out of the college building crying, he ran after me shouting verbal abuse.

When the time came to re-sit the exams, I wrote an email to the college asking them to ensure that I received extra time and the exam papers in electronic format – as had become customary for me. I wasn't surprised when the Kiwi bully called me in. This time I was prepared and secretly recorded the meeting on my phone.

"What a bitch you are! Expecting so much from a college you have done nothing for."

"The law is clear," I explained. "Reasonable adjustments need to be made for students with disabilities. This includes international students."

"Where the hell do you get your information from? Who made you the legal expert?" he boomed.

"I am happy to send the information to the college via email," I offered.

"Well, you just do that. I will not have a blind bitch like you tell me what to do. This is my college and here you and your so-called laws are nothing."

I sent the email with the information after the meeting. I also mentioned that I record all my meetings as I find it difficult to take notes and that our meeting that morning was no different. Later the same afternoon I received a reply stating that I would sit my exams at an independent invigilator in London, where I would have extra time and the exam papers in electronic format. This was a good result but it was clear that Sandy and I were no longer welcome at Fulham and Chelsea College.

Finding a new college was harder than I expected. As soon as I mentioned my visual impairment, I was told that there were no more openings available, even though their websites stated the opposite. One college even informed me that they had stairs and that I would therefore not be able to enrol there. Finally, I found a college that was willing to accommodate us: Blake Hall College in South East London near Surrey Quays. I was able to transfer only a few of my subjects and had to start virtually from scratch. But the staff had a different attitude and, although things weren't always perfect, everybody was willing to help. The college was linked to Greenwich University and I thought this would ease the process of sourcing learning materials in accessible format. Unfortunately this was not the case. The fact that I was an international student and did not have access to public funding made staff at Greenwich very reluctant to assist me.

In my final year I wrote a thesis on "Charity Branding in a Recession". Not a single textbook was available in alternative format. The most I got out of the university was an apology at the very end of the academic year. I had to source my own material, which took up a great deal of time and even a greater amount of patience. It paid off, though, and I graduated in 2011 with a 2:1 in business management.

When I first moved to London, *Big Brother* was huge and auditions for the second season had just started. Someone dared me to enter and I never say no to a dare. The first round of auditions was held in a huge shed-like hall. Thousands of hopeful applicants stood in several rows. A bunch of cheeky youngsters, obviously on power trips, was walking about, shouting instructions and placing people in different groups. I had Sandy with me so at least enjoyed some intelligent company.

As the day wore on, the people became fewer and then finally there was a change of scenery. We were taken to another shed-like room and I was asked to fill in some forms. I explained that I might need some help, and, to my surprise, they were more than willing. They even brought Sandy water and took her for walks. In fact, she was treated much better than the rest of us.

We reached a further stage where documents needed to be completed and young lady assisted me. The entire process was rather long and very tiring. Some of the questions were much stranger than I ever expected. We were also being filmed throughout the entire process – probably to see if we would throw hissy fits or if we'd make for good TV. My answers were all quite boring, until I received this question:

"What do think will would be written on your tombstone one day?" I thought for a bit and then said: "She couldn't see it coming."

I thought this was hilarious. In fact, I laughed so much, I nearly fell off my chair. I'm pretty sure the fact that I found my own answer so unequivocally amusing is what got me to the next round, and not so much the answer itself.

I made it through several rounds, but decided to withdraw. I was afraid it would interfere with my job at Guide Dogs. I'm still not sure I made the right decision, but now we'll never know.

Chapter 16: On being broken

My experience with love was not great. In London, my focus was on my career and studies. Though I had no desire to be alone, any person with a disability would agree that the dating scene is far more daunting for us than for our able-bodied counterparts. Rejection after rejection has a funny way of making you believe that you are not whole and that you have less to offer than your able-bodied peers. This was not the only factor that contributed to my lack of confidence when it came to dating and the quest for love. My religious upbringing had instilled in me the belief that only partners of the same faith would do. In such a limited environment and where there were many more young ladies than men, the guys could pick any girl they wanted. Why would they choose the 'broken' one? In my teens, not one of the lads of my faith ever showed any interest in me. In Worcester, the attention from young men outside the faith was a welcome change, but it also left me riddled with guilt – every encounter making me feel empty and lumbered with a sense of discontent.

London had its fair share of South Africans, better known as Saffas. As a result, several South African bars popped up all over to accommodate our thirsty compatriots. The two Zulu bars became a firm favourite of any Saffa in need of some sweet reminders from home. It was September 2007 when a friend and I went to the Zulu bar in Leytonstone for drinks. We'd just had dinner at the very overrated and overpriced Spur at O2. I was happy and sad at the same time. On the one hand, I had just completed a fundraising project at Guide Dogs and was over the moon about its success. On the other hand, Sandy had just retired and my four-legged miracle was no longer at my side.

Attacks on service dogs are unfortunately not uncommon. It was no different for Sandy. On our route to college, she had been attacked on several occasions by the dog of a homeless man. We did approach the police but they did not want to get involved due to a technicality regarding where the attacks took place. These attacks made Sandy nervous around other dogs and it got to a point where she could no longer focus 100 per cent on guiding me, which is why she had to retire early. Nick's parents offered to adopt her and I agreed knowing I'd be able to visit her often. Had I known this would eventually never happen, I would have been broken for life.

I was overcome with emotion and I resorted to alcohol as a temporary cure. By the time my friend and I reached the Zulu bar, I was feeling slightly better. There I met a fellow South African who came from my birth town, Pietersburg. Riaan and I hit it off immediately and the spark between us was obvious. When my friend called it a day, I decided to stay on. He had some ways to travel home but I lived not far from Leytonstone. Riaan was a true gentleman. He bought me drinks and then asked if I would like to pop outside. In the cool London night air he kissed me passionately. I had mixed emotions. Here was a true gentleman, one of my own, and interested in little old me. Someone had seen past the broken girl with her white cane and wanted more.

We kissed quite a lot and when the bar closed, Riaan asked if he could escort me home. Ah, a bloke with old-fashioned manners, just as I was raised. During the course of the evening Riaan and I had chatted about many things, including my very religious upbringing and that I was still a virgin and would remain so until the day I got married. He said he understood and distracted me with another passionate kiss. The subject came up once more while we were snogging in the cab home, and again I said that we couldn't go any further than kissing. He seemed okay with that.

Riaan asked the cabby to stop at a convenience store along the way. When we reached my flat, I invited him in for a cup of coffee, simply because it was the polite thing to do and it reflected how I was raised. I felt safe doing so because from our conversation I gathered that Riaan had been raised in much the same way. He wasn't interested in coffee, though, and produced some drinks from the blue carrier he got at the shop. He found some glasses in the kitchen and told me to sit while he poured us drinks. I knew I'd already had too much to drink but felt safe as I was home. I remember very little after that drink. I don't know when and how I got upstairs into my bed, but when I came to, Riaan was on top of me. I wanted to push him off but I could not move my arms. I wanted to ask him not to penetrate me but could hardly utter a word.

When I came to again and had enough strength to move, I found Riaan lying next to me, snoring. I woke him up and called him a taxi in the dark. Outside, I asked him what had happened. I asked him if he was inside me at all. He answered me with such pride: "I was inside you and very, very deep at that." Then he got into his cab and left.

I went back to my room, still dazed and confused. I switched on the light and nearly fainted with shock. My bedding was smeared with blood.

The first thing I felt was guilt – an all-consuming feeling of guilt, that this was all my fault. Why had I been in the pub in the first place? Why was I even flirting with a man who was not of the same faith? How could I let this happen? I had lost my virginity out of wedlock and I was in trouble. As soon as daylight broke and it was a reasonable hour, I phoned the church elders to confess my sin and seek support. My second greatest fear was that I might be pregnant. One of the elders sent his wife who took me to a pharmacy to get a pregnancy test. The morning after pill was out of the question as it was considered an abortion that was strictly forbidden. I was completely lost. I called my former landlady in Beckenham. She was on holiday but said I could stay at her home for a few days. It wasn't until three days after it had happened that I spoke to Yolandi, a fellow South African who lived across the road in Brunel Street. She listened intently, then took my hand and said, "Theresa, you were raped."

Over the next two days, I reached out to five different people – all church members I had looked up to and felt would support me in this hour of need. They were not related in any way, but all five had exactly the same reply: "Well, I hope this is a wakeup call for you. You are spiritually weak and this is what happens if you're not spiritually strong. If you were stronger and more active in the church, this would not have happened."

I called the elder I'd spoken to the morning after it had happened again. I will never forget his reply on the phone.

"I am an elder in the congregation. It is my duty to make sure you live according to Biblical principles and to protect the congregation from those who stray from the path. I firmly believe there is no such thing as rape. Women put themselves in situations they should never have been in, by the places they go and the clothes they wear. I am not interested in hearing about your cry of rape. What I want to know is, why did you go to that bar and mingle with worldly people? Why did you allow a non-believer to kiss you and then walk you home?

"Your situation is a result of your bad choices, and for that we need to put you in front of a judicial committee and decide on a suitable way to reprimand you. We need to protect the congregation from you, until such time as you have shown an improvement in your life choices and have made an effort to increase activity within the faith. You are to be blamed for what happened because you ignored the Biblical principles you have been taught, such as to avoid bad associations and places of ill-repute.

"Your request for comfort and support is absurd as what happened to you is entirely your fault. You cannot expect fellow worshippers to love and support you if you are now a bad association yourself. At our next meeting a public announcement will be made that you are under public reproof and that members in the congregation should refrain from spending time with you. Your request for someone to accompany you in going to the police and a doctor is absurd. You need to deal with the consequences of your actions by yourself and not burden fellow members with it.

"Your spiritual activities over the past few years have been lacking, with few hours preaching and poor attendance at meetings. We believe this has made you spiritually weak and resulted in your current predicament. You are a disappointment to your family who is strong in the faith. You have been raised on Biblical principles. Let us hope you can return to better ways."

Never in my entire life had I felt more lonely, lost and afraid than I did at that moment. I was utterly stunned by his response. At a complete loss and not knowing whom to turn to, I found myself dialling the number of Nikki, my manager. I told her what had happened and how afraid and guilty I felt. She was at my door mere minutes after our call. She calmly put her arms around me and told me that it was not my fault. After several cups of tea and copious tears, she encouraged me to report the matter to the police. Two officers arrived at my home the next day, one male and one female. I remember watching the young officer. He most certainly did not believe a word I said. I confronted him about this and he merely shrugged his shoulders. They took down my statement and then explained that I would have to be examined by a police doctor and interviewed again at the station.

Although the UK system for supporting victims of sexual assault is good, their forms are not accessible to people who are visually impaired. After the ordeal of an internal exam and reliving the trauma by recounting the incident to yet another official, and again to several different officers, I was sent home. I was shattered and in a terrible state. No one from my church would accompany me to the police station or the hospital. They didn't believe it was rape so I was not entitled to their time. That evening my phone rang. It was someone from the police station where I had reported my rape. The man on the other side of the phone asked casually, "Is this Miss Robberts?"

"Yes," I replied.

"I had a look at your case file. We both know that no rape took place here, so let's just call it a day, shall we?"

"No, no, I was raped!" I managed to get out through the tears.

"Fine then, we'll be in touch." The phone went dead.

A week later, I had a visit from a much kinder policewoman. I told her I had decided to drop the case. As I had reported it only three days after the event, there was no forensic evidence left and no trace in my blood of whatever had been put in my drink that night.

There is much to be learnt during trying times. Whom you can count on for support and unconditional love is part of it. Two days after my nightmare, I called my brother André and told him everything. André was on the next plane to London and accompanied me to all the follow-up appointments I had with police and doctors the following week. Although he was also part of the faith, he never judged me and the only issue that I had with him was that I had to make sure he did not find out where Riaan lived. The last thing we needed was him being on the wrong side of the law.

Unbeknown to me at the time, André had been dealing with his own struggles. He was married to Nicole, a woman I did not get along with at the best of times. André loved her, though, and I respected their relationship. Nicole and her family were obviously in the same faith, but for them it was all or nothing – everything was black and white. I found Nicole and her family to be some of the most judgemental people I had ever met. The tabloid press had nothing on them. She treated my brother like some sort of trophy. He was expected to set an example within the congregation. There was no room for him to be himself and nothing he did was ever good enough. Whenever I visited them, their family discussion would be about some or other person or family who did not live up to their standards.

While he was married to Nicole, André met another girl, Amanda. I do not support divorce, but his leaving Nicole and her family saved his life. He was practically falling apart under their control. With Amanda, the happy, kind-hearted man I had always known him to be was back. André is still part of the faith but I have great respect for him as, unlike most, he loves and respects others. He is not judgemental. Because we don't agree about everything does not mean we can't have respect for one another, and yes, believe it or not, love one another. If all the members of the faith were like André, I'd be back in a heartbeat.

London opened my mind to so many things. There had been many instances leading up to this, but the way in which the people of our faith had treated me after my sexual assault finally lead me to leave. Though love was said to be one of the cornerstones of our faith, I found the members completely lacking in love for one another. Instead, I found them judgemental to the extreme. I knew this was a great disappointment to my parents, especially my dad. His faith is his life and I love and respect him for this so very much. It was, however, not for me.

Chapter 17: I kissed a girl and I liked it

When you move away from certain beliefs and viewpoints, it naturally opens the door to others. In my case, these new views were not religious as such. Leaving the faith simply helped me stop being the judgemental person that I was. Instead, I gave everyone a chance and a place to be.

This change in thought and beliefs had another unexpected effect. Not long after I joined Guide Dogs, something very unusual began to happen. Each time Devina, my manager at the time, entered the office, my heart went aflutter and my palms began to sweat. Since she was a woman, my reaction confused me. It was as scary as it was exciting. I felt like a teenager experiencing a first crush all over again. I couldn't stop looking at her legs. I was reminded of Miss Swart, my Phys. Ed. teacher at Prinshof. She, too, had amazing legs and back then I thought all the girls had been admiring her legs as much as I did.

Devina was married and straight as an arrow. I believe she was unaware of my admiration. I put it down to a passing phase. As soon as she announced that she was pregnant, my crush disappeared as quickly as it had manifested itself. I was equally relieved and disappointed. I decided it was for the best and thought nothing more of it until the day our new manager, Nikki, walked into the office. Fireworks! She was mind-blowingly beautiful. We worked on several projects together, including a couple of Jailbreaks. She was a great manager and also became a lifelong, trusted friend. When so many of my support pillars crumbled after the sexual assault, Nikki took their place. She was there for me during that trying time and continues to be a rock-solid friend to this day.

She had come to know me quite well and maybe saw things that I couldn't see. During lunch one day, quite matter-of-factly, she suggested that I might be bi-curious.

"Bi-curious? What on earth is that?" I asked.

She explained and then made a few suggestions on how I could look into it further. I'll never forget her saying: "We need to get you out there Tee, in a safe way."

I had no idea what she meant but I trusted her so I listened intently.

Most of what she told me made me blush profusely. I blush ridiculously easily, sometimes for no reason at all, and this time it felt like my ears were on fire.

"Because of the sexual assault, you will have very little confidence with anything of a sexual nature. To get that confidence back, you should get a rabbit."

"I can't have a pet where I live and Rikki will think it's the perfect toy."

"No Tee, not a bunny, a rabbit sex toy."

"What? I've never heard of a sex toy, never mind one called a rabbit."

Nikki decided a practical lesson would be best and so off we went to Soho to a well-known sex shop. This was my second experience of something akin to a red-light district. London might have a red-light district, but nothing was glowing a brighter red than my face and ears. Nikki was well-trained in providing sighted-guidance to blind people so she did not just point to a toy on the shelf. She asked if I could hold a demo model and the manager complied with a cheeky smile. I still did not understand how this vibrating rubber thing, which looked nothing like a rabbit by the way, would help me. I stood there thinking and feeling like my mother could walk in at any moment, although she was thousands of miles away. I was mortified.

Next stop was the sex bookshop. Nikki suggested that one of the safest ways to explore my interest in girls would be to read erotic short stories and see if they had any effect on me.

"I certainly don't think so!" I said confidently.

Nikki wasn't one to give up so I eventually gave up protesting and chose a book filled with erotic, girl-on-girl travel stories.

"At least the travel side of the stories will interest me," I said.

Two weeks later, it was my 30th birthday and my gift from Nikki was a rabbit, not of the furry kind. That Sunday evening I locked my bedroom door, closed the curtains and cautiously opened the box. I vaguely recalled an incident a colleague had shared. Her friend lived with her parents in a ground-floor bedroom next to the living room. She had some sort of sex toy. She was rather spoiled and her mum made her bed each morning. One such morning, she realised with a blush that she had left her toy amongst the sheets. Her mum was bound to make this embarrassing discovery. As she entered the house after work, she hurried over to her mum.

"Thanks for making my bed, Mum."

"No problem darling," her mum said, without looking up from her ironing.

"I am really sorry that you had to find my er … my um …"

"Oh that!" her mum interrupted and looked at her with a cheeky grin.

"Your dad and I are well aware of your toys darling. Have been for a while. Every time you use one, it interferes with the signal on the telly."

I was not ready for that level of embarrassment. What would my housemates think of me? The shame! The rabbit was even bigger than it looked in the shop. As usual, the instructions were in microscopic print. I did not have access to the Internet and there was no way I could ask my housemates to assist. I was scared and curious at the same time. I looked at the monster rabbit and thought, "There is no way this massive piece of silicon will go inside me." I then focused my attention on the small, vibrating bits on the side. Curiosity overcame fear and feelings of guilt and thank goodness it did. The product got an A+ from me.

The short stories were another agreeable surprise. Nikki was right, I must be bi-curious. I searched the Internet and found a group for bi-curious people that met in Euston. When I got to the venue, Rikki and I made our way up a very tricky, steel, spiral staircase. After we'd found a spot and settled, I realised how formal and quiet everything seemed. It soon became clear we were not in the right place. We had, in fact, just joined a Buddhist meeting. I did not want to disrupt the meeting by getting up and leaving. Instead, in the middle of it all, I disrupted the meeting when my phone went off, blaring out a South African rugby anthem ringtone. I might not have been able to see the looks I was receiving, but I could most certainly feel them. Rikki and I used this embarrassing moment to make our exit. The group that I was looking for was downstairs. All they did was have drinks and socialise. Everyone seemed to know one another and I felt a bit like the odd one out. Just before we left, a dark-haired Mediterranean goddess approached me. With a strong, sultry accent she asked, "What you doing here?"

"I'm here because I think I'm bisexual."

She was daunting and beautiful all at once. She looked at me with piercing dark eyes and said, "You're not, you're gay."

And, with that, she left. How would she know anything about me? I decided to treat this as nothing more than a brief encounter with a beautiful Spanish goddess, and left it at that.

Exploring this new side of me was as exhilarating as it was unnerving. My entire life I had been taught how wrong this was. And yet now it felt so completely natural. I was worried that what I was experiencing was driven more by the trauma of my sexual assault than my actual feelings; that being attracted to women made me feel safe because it helped me avoid men. I decided I needed to know. I started dating a South African lad 10 years my junior. We had sex several times but I still found it wanting. I put my lack of excitement down to his lack of experience and moved on. After a few affairs, I finally met the 'perfect' guy and, with that, found the 'perfect' situation. He was a professional windsurfer, tanned with long bleach-blonde hair. He was absolutely 'my type'. He was quite experienced and took me to a yacht whose owners were away. The fact that they could return at any moment added to my overall excitement. He picked me up and, with my legs wrapped around him, he had me in what I always thought would be my favourite position. While he was passionately and enthusiastically doing his thing, I remember looking over his shoulder, bored out of my mind.

When I discussed this with Nikki she said, "Your Spanish goddess was right. I knew from the start you were gay and so did Nick, but telling you that from the word go would have scared the hell out of you." For some time after that I was still not 100 per cent convinced. It took my first kiss from a girl to make the penny drop.

Nikki became my best friend and accompanied me through a turbulent time of fear, heartache, excitement and discovery. My crush on her evolved very quickly into a deep-seated love. But like Devina, Nikki was straight and I had to find a way to deal with this. I decided the best thing to do would be to tell her. We went for a meal and a very nervous me plucked up the courage to tell her.

"Nikki, I'm not expecting you to do anything about this as I know nothing can come of it, but I need you to know I'm in love with you."

Casually, while stealing chips off my plate, Nikki said, "Oh, okay." And that was that. I was able to move on and the Scottish lass and I are still good friends today.

Chapter 18: A rainbow rollercoaster

London was the perfect place to come out of the closet. There are so many social groups you can join. The first all-female social group I joined was Ladies to Dine For. We'd get together once a month at different restaurants of our choosing. It was here that I met Thuy, a French biologist of Vietnamese descent. She was tiny in stature but a force to be reckoned with. We'd been introduced to each other at a few of these get-togethers, but I really got to chat to her for the first time only at a Christmas do.

Thuy studied bacteria and, as a result, was a complete hygiene freak. Each time I arrived at her flat, she would hand me a pair of tracksuit pants. I was allowed to sit only once I had these on.

"Public transport is filthy," she explained.

Thuy was the first girl I had sex with. It was her first time too, so it was a clumsy, awkward affair. I still thought it was amazing. Thuy's obsession with hygiene did put a slight damper on the romance though, as I had to follow a strict shower and scrub regimen both before and after each time we shared a bed. Deep down, I knew she was not 'the one' but, as with most things in life, I gave it my all. As it turned out, my all was a little too much and Thuy broke up with me a few months later.

Next up was online dating. I used several sites and went on quite a few dates. I met some wonderful, but mostly very weird, girls this way. Like Sophie. We met on a site specifically for lesbians and from the word go we got on like a house on fire. Sophie was not a boring, one-liner communicator. Oh no! We exchanged long, emotion-filled paragraphs. Her sense of humour was spot on and I was hooked.

Our online chats continued for a few months before we finally arranged our first date. Sophie was a professional bodyguard and Sharon Stone was one of her clients. She was my age and lived in Bedfordshire, about two hours' travel by train away. A very excited Rikki and I hopped on a train late one Saturday afternoon to meet Sophie. She met us at the station and I have to admit, I was quite shocked when I first saw her. Sophie did not look like her online photo. Three of those Sophies could fit into the body of the Sophie who stood before us. Nevertheless we got in her car and were on our way. I am a firm believer in not judging a book by its cover and I was determined not to let the revelation of Sophie's size put me off. After all, we had had some great chats online and I was dying to get to know this woman better.

The trip in the car was really quiet, but I put the awkward silence down to nerves. When we arrived at her home, we met her very large and very friendly Rottweiler, Rotty. Unlike Sophie and I, Rikki and Rotty were completely at ease with each other. Rikki must have thought she had just walked into paradise as Sophie's home was filled with dog toys. She really had a glorious evening. I on the other hand, not so much. In person, Sophie was a completely different person and nothing like the woman I had met online. Her ability to have any kind of conversation mysteriously disappeared and trying to talk to her was actually hard work.

"Do you have any brothers or sisters?" I asked, attempting to find the online version of Sophie.

"Yes," she replied, coldly.

"A sister?"

"Yes."

"Two sisters?"

"No."

"Oh, a brother and a sister?"

"Yes."

"Do you get along with them?"

"No."

Getting responses from her was like pulling teeth, but I persevered and learnt that Sophie had hurt her shoulder six years before while on duty. Since then, she'd been off sick and on benefits.

The evening dragged on. After two hours of this and a few uncomfortable silences, Sophie finally said something. To my surprise, it was a question and it consisted of more than just one word.

"I think we must get a takeaway. Is Indian okay for you?"

"Perfect!" I said. Even I could deliver the odd, one-word sentence.

She bought an enormous amount of food. The three of us, Sophie, Rotty and I (in that order) sat on her black leather couch. She balanced her plate, stacked with food, on her chest and shovelled it all in. Then she went back for seconds and thirds. At the end of her feast, she hauled out two bags of jelly babies. She offered me some. I took two and watched as she scoffed down the rest.

As with any good Chinese takeaway, it came with a bag of prawn crackers. This was the one thing that Sophie did not eat. It was a special treat for Rotty. He wolfed them down while lying sprawled out between us on the fancy leather couch. He fell asleep with his head on Sophie's lap and his bum pointing my way. It was not long before the prawn-cocktail farts hit me. I nearly died from that smell.

Sophie then mentioned that she'd made an anniversary card for an ex-partner's parents. She wanted to hand-deliver the card that evening and asked if we'd like to come along. I agreed, just happy that I got two sentences out of the woman. She told us to wait in the car while she quickly dropped off the card. It must have been a very long journey from the garden gate to the front door. Sophie returned to the car an hour and a half later.

I am a very optimistic person but even I had to declare the date a disaster. At least Rikki had a great time. It was too late to travel back to London so we stayed the night. The next day, Sophie took us back to the train station. There was no conversation in the car (surprise, surprise!). What followed next was a bit of a shocker, though: she dropped us on a dual-carriageway on the opposite side to the station. She said that parking on the station side would just be too much trouble. Rikki and I have always loved a challenge, but crossing several lanes of traffic on our own was not on our list of must-do, adrenaline-filled activities. I never heard from Sophie again.

After numerous other unsuccessful dates and a disastrous speed dating experience, I finally seemed to have hit the jackpot. I met Sharon. She was a few years older than me and bore a slight resemblance to Roxette's Marie Fredrickson, who had been a lifetime crush of mine. This counted very much in Sharon's favour.

Not long after we met online, Sharon and I met in person one Sunday evening at a gay pub in Soho. She looked just like her profile picture. Thank God! I was hooked. She was slender with short, spiky, light blonde hair. When we kissed, rockets went off in my head. Sharon had so much more experience than I did when it came to women. She was ready to share and I was ready to learn.

On our second date, only a few days later, we met at the same pub at Soho Square. We kissed for ages and, when we stopped, she looked at me and asked, "So, are you taking me home or not?"

For the next few months, I was on a mind-blowing, orgasmic journey. Many of the erotic short stories I had read were now playing themselves out in my life. There was one thing missing though. We always met at my place. Sharon still lived with her ex and that complicated things. Sharon made a very good living in comparison to my limited income on a student visa.

She treated me to an amazing weekend at Brighton Pride. Rikki was given the weekend off and went to stay with Desiré and Monique. Sharon had booked us into a stunning B&B owned by two friendly guys. When we arrived that Friday, we explored the streets of Brighton. The weather was gorgeous and the mojitos even better. We didn't see much of the rest of Brighton or any of the festivities that weekend and decided instead to make the most of our very luxurious accommodation.

It all seemed too perfect and for the most part I was walking around grinning like a Cheshire cat. I saw a future with Sharon even though she remained distant when the conversation went that way. One day, not long after the Pride weekend, she stopped returning my calls and I never heard from her again.

At first I was really worried that something had happened to her. I could not contact any of her friends or relatives as I had never met any of them. I should have read the signs. Although Sharon was with me, her heart was not. She was still in love with her ex and, in time, I learnt that her ex was no longer her ex – I was.

One would have thought that I had finally made peace with the fact that I was gay, but it's much easier said than done. I was desperate not to be lonely and I was in need of kindness in my life. Amit was a gentleman who played cricket with us. Over time, he slowly crept into my heart. He was sincere and caring, unlike most men I had known. I considered that maybe I was just expecting too much: a romantic, physical relationship filled with kindness and compassion. Maybe I should forget about the romance and the spark and settle for kindness.

Amit and I started dating. This was a huge mistake on my part.

He was 100 per cent committed and I believe he was in love with me. He was such a gentle soul who had my best interests at heart. I could not continue with the relationship and I broke his heart. To this day, I feel ashamed of what I did to him and no amount of apologising will ever make up for the hurt I caused him. Staying with Amit would also have been the wrong choice but I should never have started the relationship in the first place.

In my search for 'the one' I met a girl called Hayley. She was younger than me, blind, and had a guide dog called Una. I admired Hayley tremendously. She was a very successful career woman and had accomplished so much. I always envied the way she could apply make-up and cook. She was born blind, yet she was brilliant at doing these things. Hayley and I were never in a proper relationship. After a few dates she realised it was not what she was looking for and I respected her choice. We remained friends and I spent the next Christmas with her and her housemate. Oh my goodness, the woman could cook! Hayley met her one-and-only shortly afterwards – a South African lass no less. We are irresistible.

I met Diane in early 2012. A fellow South African, she was also blind and played cricket. She was based in Brighton and joined us for the monthly coaching sessions with her guide dog, Thomas. We called him Lord Thomas. He was a large yellow lab with an attitude and kept his nose in the air most of the time.

Diane lost her eyesight when she contracted meningitis in her twenties. She was rushed to hospital but the doctor who treated her gave her the wrong medication. The result was that she went in fully sighted and woke up completely blind. She ended up moving to the UK as she was entitled to a British passport. Diane was a feisty woman who did not hold back when it came to standing up for her rights as a disabled person. This made her a brilliant activist but not always that easy to live with.

Diane and I had too much in common not to fall in love. It was the start of a relationship lasting much longer that any of my previous ones. Many weekends Rikki and I would hop on a train at Victoria and make our way down to Brighton to visit Diane and Thomas. We had some great times visiting coffee shops, taking the dogs to the beach or just chilling at home. When our relationship was still very new and the passion was high, I approached her while she was cooking in the kitchen. I stood behind her and wrapped my arms around her. What I did then had the desired effect as she dropped what she was busy doing, turned around and kissed me passionately. The kitchen floor was soon covered in our clothes. Diane snaked her fingers inside me and I received them gladly until all of a sudden an incredible stinging pain jolted me back to reality. I closed my eyes and prayed it would pass but it only got worse. I let go of Diane and explained my sudden lack of interest. She stood perplexed for a few seconds and then a cheeky grin appeared on her face. She tried to hide it but couldn't and had to confess: "Oh dear babe, I've been cooking with chillies!" My mind worked overtime. In a flash of brilliance, I grabbed Thomas' Johnson's Baby shampoo and rushed to the shower. "No more tears" got a whole new meaning that day.

I was convinced that I would someday marry Diane, but when I casually mentioned to her that if I couldn't get a work permit, the only way for me to stay in the UK would be to get married, my comment did not go down well at all.

We had been together for about a year and a half when I became ill with a fistula that left me bedridden for weeks. During that time, Diane never came to visit me. When I asked her why, she was furious that I had even asked. The next time we went to visit her she ended our relationship.

Diane suffered from back pain. Her back always troubled her when we played cricket and eventually she had to stop playing altogether. She finally went for a long overdue back operation later that year. Over the phone, she informed me that according to her doctor I was to blame.

“How can I be to blame for your back pain when I’m not even near you?”

“The emotional strain you caused me with your illness put me under a lot of pressure, which caused my back pain.”

I was dumbfounded. Did she really believe this? Apparently she did. I don’t break contact deliberately with many people, but in this case I did.

It was only back in South Africa that I would find love again.

Chapter 19: Rikki - another four-legged miracle

There is a Chinese saying: "First the egg has to crack before the bird can fly". I honestly believe that traumatic experiences are followed by wonderful, life-changing events. All you need to do is to be open for them and ready to take off. After the sexual assault and a subsequent mental breakdown, my life took a different turn. I was paired with my second guide dog, Rikki. Like Sandy, she was a beautiful yellow lab, but with a black blotch at the base of her tail. Passers-by would often stop me to let me know that my dog had sat in something like paint or tar. Rikki was my second miracle. She was raised as a puppy in Norway, trained by a Scotsman called Rick, and now had a South African mum: a truly international pup. She helped me gradually get my confidence back. I had a choice to make: stay at home, afraid and scared; or go out and live. Once I made the choice, wonderful things began to happen.

I decided to get active and fill my weekends and evenings with something I am passionate about: sport. Sport is a great love of mine. At school I was not allowed to participate – my parents forbade it and, in my early twenties, the shock of losing my sight kept me imprisoned in my own home. Sandy, my first guide dog, gave me the courage to realise my dream to live abroad. Rikki gave me newfound confidence to get involved in sport instead of fading away as a spectator on the couch. My online research pointed me to the Metro Sports club for the blind. I had certainly hit gold.

The club was run by visually-impaired sports enthusiasts and had a wide variety of sporting options on offer. When I joined, my first choice was blind tennis. With a few adaptations, this thrilling sport has become accessible to visually-impaired athletes. The court and net are normal except that a slightly smaller area is used, and indoor courts are better suited. The ball is slightly bigger and made of a sponge-like material that makes it bounce and travel more slowly than a regular tennis ball would. In the middle of the ball is a smaller ball with a couple of ball bearings. These create a rattling sound when the ball moves. Players use a short-handled racquet and are allowed to let the ball bounce twice. They can even compete against sighted players who then get only one bounce.

I remember my first evening joining some Metro members to have a go. In the changing rooms I felt so shy and self-conscious. It almost felt like being back at school. The girls looked fit and healthy and they were chattering away while I nervously got dressed at a frantic pace. I was so anxious I almost left, but I am so very happy that I didn't. On court, everyone was very helpful and I soon felt part of this happy, chattering active group of friends. I loved playing blind tennis and started going to practice sessions on Friday evenings. While living in England, I played in the national tournament every year. I came second, beaten only by French Odette each time in the singles. I won the women's doubles one year with Amanda as partner and the mixed doubles with Matt another year.

I got to meet a special couple – Heindrich and Anchen who were also from South Africa but by that time had been living in the UK for over 20 years. He was a physio and had trained in the UK after leaving school. He was one of the best all-time blind cricketers in England and probably the world. I always listened with envy as he spoke about the weekend ahead and the cricket games they were scheduled to play. One evening at tennis practice, I overheard him mentioning to someone that they were short a few players for the next days' match.

"Pity the girls can't play!" I blurted out.

"Yes they can," he said.

"But you don't have any girls playing do you?" I asked.

"No, we don't, but that doesn't mean they can't. We had a very good female team member a few years back. Would you like to join?"

"Hell yes! But I've never played before. It would be scary."

"As if anything scares you! You are, after all, a Blue Bull." (We both supported the same South African rugby team.) He had me there. My slight hesitation gave him a gap.

"We meet at Waterloo Station at 6:30am on platform one. I'll let Rory, the captain, know he has one less player to worry about."

That night I hardly slept but Rikki and I were at Waterloo at 6am.

Blind cricket, like blind tennis, is very similar to the sighted version. Again, the ball is the biggest difference. A hard, white, hollow Perspex ball is used. Although it is more or less the same size as a normal cricket ball, it is filled with bearings that create a rattling noise. The same field is used but the stumps are a different colour to make them more visible. Communication plays a vital part in this sport. Keepers, in particular, need a good strong voice to indicate, first for the bowler where the stumps are, and then to the fielders when throwing the ball in. That day, I was pretty dismal on the field yet I felt like a million bucks. I was part of the team. Yes, they were all men, but it hardly mattered: I wanted more.

It was on that day that I met Rory Field, captain of the Metro team. Rory was a South African but, like Hein, had been living in the UK for a long time. Like me, Rory had tunnel vision and it was partly due to this that he met the lovely Nina, who later became his wife. Rory is a tall bloke and Nina a short, German girl. She was walking with her umbrella blocking her view in the pouring rain and Rory did not spot her way down there. The result was a collision followed by profuse apologies, which was then followed by a coffee. The rest, as they say, is history.

Metro turned out to have a very strong team with a proud history of producing international players, year after year. Qualifying for the team was hard. For the first season, I was twelfth man at most games but I still loved it. I also made sandwiches for the two competing teams' lunches when we had a home match. I would fill my 'coffin' to the brim with lunch packs, drinks and cricket gear. A cricket kit bag is often referred to as a coffin because of its size and possibly also because it weighs as much as a dead body. Mine fitted on my back, not very comfortably, but it enabled me to carry it and still have my hands free to be guided by Rikki. Our home ground was located in Highgate Woods. It was beautiful, but could only be reached by a short walk through the woods, which was usually wet and muddy. On a particularly slippery day, Rikki and I made our way to the field via the muddy path. Suddenly, I slipped and did a faceplant in a huge puddle of muddy water. With the coffin on my back, getting up was hard.

Rikki looked at me like I had gone mad and then had a very mischievous look in her eyes. She promptly flopped down in the muddy puddle next to me and buried her nose in it. She was elated to discover that we both loved mud. Just as I was about to find my way up, she shook the mud from her coat, adding it to mine.

Away-games were fun too. Early mornings at a London station, with a Costa coffee in hand, 12 to 14 blindies boarded the train with a couple of guide dogs in tow. We always asked railway staff for assistance and many times we would be moved to first class to make things easier. Just one of the many perks of being visually impaired.

I will never forget a game we played in Southend. In blind cricket, the B1 players (those with no sight) have a runner who runs on their behalf between the wickets. Our team batted second and I was asked to be a runner for one of our players. I was so focused. Looking straight ahead, bat in hand, I waited for the call from the other batsman. It came and I was off like a shot. Because of my tunnel vision, I could not see what was going on to the sides of the pitch – I did not need to – I only needed to get to the other side of the pitch. The player from the opposing team, fielding at this point, also had tunnel vision. He, too, heard the ball and ran straight ahead. Our running paths were at a right angle and we smashed into one another at full speed. After a brief moment, I came to my senses and was pretty chuffed with what I saw. My opponent looked a mess with broken spectacles and a deep cut requiring stitches on his lip. I, on the other hand, was just fine. I carried on playing for a bit but a headache and fatigue forced me to take a break. As I walked off the pitch, I collapsed before I reached the boundary. An ambulance was called. When I opened my eyes, I was on a stretcher in the back of the ambulance with two paramedics and Rikki at my side. I spent the night in A&E with a concussion. Fortunately, Dom, one of my teammates, stayed with me and looked after Rikki.

The Metro team grew and soon there were several of us who rarely got match time. The club then decided to start a development team. We called it the Metro Devils, taking the dev from development. This was a great idea and meant that everyone had a chance to play. We also had more girls joining because this group was a bit less intimidating. The UK now has a development league and most counties enter their teams. I know some of the guys started out playing for the Devils and later became part of the national squad.

I am eternally grateful that Hein convinced me to give blind cricket a go. I met many amazing people and had great opportunities as a result. Hein became a mentor and an inspiration in my life. He and his life partner, Anchen, were always there to encourage and support me. Hein and I got on so well, always having a natter about our favourite rugby teams.

One morning, just before the start of a tennis tournament, one of the players called me aside.

"Hein and Anchen went on holiday to a resort in Morocco but Hein did not come back," she said with tears in her eyes.

"Why?" I asked, not fully understanding.

"Hein went to swim some lengths at the resort gym pool one morning and came back feeling tired," she continued.

"He went to lie down and started feeling worse. There were no doctors at the resort and by the time help was found, Hein was dead. He had suffered a heart attack."

The room spun and I sat down in shock and disbelief.

"I don't get it! He was in his early forties; a strong, healthy man."

The death of Heindrich Swanepoel shook the disabled sporting community, not just in the UK but all over the world. He was a superstar, both on and off the field. I still miss him sorely.

Chapter 20: Bowled over by blind cricket

I had been playing cricket for some time when I heard about Beth Evans who had started coaching a group of girls in Surrey. I was ecstatic to hear about this and made contact. Soon I joined their training session on certain Saturdays. It was a long trip from where I lived in London, but absolutely worth it. Beth was amazing. She was a sighted girl with a great love of cricket who was ready to share her knowledge and enthusiasm.

Most of the girls who participated were young enough to be my daughters but that did not matter. They kept me going and I made some amazing friends. Sarah was one of them. I met her at one of our training sessions with Beth. She had just acquired her first guide dog, Jess, a golden retriever. Jess and Rikki became great chums, too, as we travelled and played cricket together over the next few years. It's a good thing these two furry girls could not talk as they were also present when we got up to a lot of mischief. It was amazing to see how Jess transformed Sarah's life – from being quiet and shy with low self-confidence to getting a great job and travelling the world. Sarah also got a place of her own which happened to be in the lodge where I lived. Sarah now lives in Bristol, organises huge fundraising events for worthy causes and is an inspiration to many.

It's great to see how many females are participating in blind cricket, not just in the UK, but all over the globe. Nepal, for instance, has a full, all-female national team. After years of hard work and perseverance, Beth made a dream turn into reality for me, Sarah and nine other visually-impaired women. In October 2014 we took on Nepal on their home ground in the first all-female international blind cricket tournament.

Every moment of this trip was an adventure. Even the long, bumpy bus rides were priceless. The girls would sing along to music, chat and laugh. Steve and Jacqueline, our team managers, and Si our physio, joined us. Our tour started in the north of Nepal and we trained on a very rugged outfield and pitch every day. I felt like I was in heaven. This time I was not only wearing team kit, this time we even had our surnames emblazoned on the back of our shirts. We played in bright pink and navy. Even our shoes were bright pink and we looked fabulous. In the evenings we went out for meals and bonded as a group. We also took in the sights of this amazing country. I loved the people of Nepal and found them to be incredibly kind and gentle. I did not know very much about Buddhism prior to this trip, but seeing how peaceful followers of this religion were gave me much food for thought.

After our training sessions up north, we travelled back to the capital Kathmandu. The traffic coupled with how people drove was nerve-wracking to experience, even for a bunch of blindies. Even scarier though, was the Press. The tournament we were about to play had caught the media's attention and there were cameras everywhere. Our support teams had their hands full. At one point they literally had to pull a cameraman away from pushing his camera into the face of one of our youngest players.

When our first match-day finally arrived, the excitement in the air was tangible. We were sitting next to the field doing warm-up exercises with Si and were surrounded by cameras. Then I felt it. A big fart inside of me, nagging to be let out. "Please let this be a silent one," I prayed. It was not. Drrrr! It ripped out! Everyone stopped. All the girls started laughing and pointing to poor Sarah who was sitting next to me. She pleaded her innocence and after letting her suffer a little while longer I eventually stepped in and confessed. I do hope this was never broadcast, but I'll never be entirely sure. I'm forever grateful, though, that I never suffered from Delhi belly as so many of the other girls did. That would have been a disaster.

The pitch we played on that day was entirely different from the one we had been practising on throughout the tour. It was smooth and rock solid. I'm convinced it was made of concrete or something similar. We might have lost all three matches but we walked away winners. It was the experience of a lifetime. I still wonder if Beth ever realised exactly what an incredible impact she had on all our lives.

Chapter 21: Sporting brilliance

When I joined Metro, I met Amanda Green, one of the club's committee members and also a blind sailing enthusiast. Sailing was very new to me, but again, I had to give it a go. One could participate in different types of sailing events – trips on large sailing boats on the English Channel, or to the Isle of Man, or racing the smaller dinghies. My first experience was on a 60-ft yacht called the Donald Searl. It was crewed by 22 people, 11 sighted and 11 blindies. I remember getting stuck in and working really hard on this trip. I loved it. We had strong wind, which made for great sailing. It also allowed me to indulge my wicked sense of humour while I was at the helm. I once waited until the crew were working in the kitchen preparing potatoes and then keeled the boat – all the spuds went flying. I might not have been very popular at that moment but found this hilarious. Nikki joined me on this trip but didn't quite find her sea legs. For most of the trip her face was an odd shade of green and I think she much preferred being on dry land.

Sailing on the smaller boats was an entirely different story. Usually, we were three to a boat, including one completely blind person. In sporting terminology they are classed as a B1. Then there would be a B2, like me, or a B3 with partial vision working on the jibs. The third person is a sighted tactician who is not allowed to touch anything, only to communicate with the helm. I took part in the British national sailing championships and twice received a silver medal in my category. My favourite tournament was one during which I was teamed up with Abby, a B1 also living at the lodge, and Charley. Charley was an experienced young sailor who brightened up the day wherever she went. We aptly named ourselves Charley's Angels for the duration of the tournament. The world absolutely needs more people like Charley; it was utterly heart-breaking when she lost her battle to cancer shortly before turning 30.

While playing tennis and cricket, I realised that I if I wanted to become a better player, I'd need to increase my fitness level. I started running. I am not a natural runner so this was never going to be easy. I did mostly 5km runs and once in a blue moon a 10km. In 2009, Nikki suggested that I sign up for the London Marathon. I guess it helped that I loved the girl so much. If anyone else had suggested it, I would have shoved them and their silly ideas off a cliff. But it was Nikki and she offered to be my guide runner. Spending hours of training each day seemed that much more alluring when your training partner happened to be gorgeous. Ignoring my head and all common sense, I followed my heart and signed up. Two months later, Nikki had to move back to Scotland to look after her gran after her granddad passed away. She could no longer be my guide runner or even a good-looking training buddy.

I had made the commitment, though, and decided to stick to it. Desiré and Monique helped with training at weekends by doing long runs in the bitterly cold weather with me. Desiré, bless her, is not the best of guides (to put it mildly) and on more than one occasion had me crashing into wheelie bins. Carol, a good friend who was also from South Africa, volunteered to be my guide for the marathon. It would be her first marathon too.

The training was hard and extremely time-consuming. For at least three to four months I had no social life. But the experience on the day made every minute worth it. It was suggested that we print our names on the front of our shirts so that spectators could know who we were, and it worked. Getting cheered from the side is great, but hearing your name too is such a boost. All along the route, people were cheering and spurring us on. Well, everyone except some idiot who shouted a nasty comment about my breasts. I stopped in my tracks and marched over towards where the comment had come from. I did not see him as he quickly disappeared. Obviously he had not expected the blind athlete to try to find him.

Carol and I ran with a band connecting us and she was always half a step ahead of me, informing other runners in no uncertain terms that a blind runner was approaching. I have since done many races but now I prefer to run with my white cane. I'm not sure if it's simply because I am stubborn, but I find it works better for me. Except, of course, when the road is pock-marked with potholes. Fellow runners often recognise me at park-runs and other organised events. I guess you can call me the cane runner. I think it's great since our country no longer has a blade runner, we might just as well settle for a cane runner. The cane runner might not be as fast as the blade runner but at least she won't be shooting anyone anytime soon.

Metro also hosts a blind athletics championships each year and I even had a go at that. Javelin was a mess as I kept on stepping over the line, but I managed silver medals in discus and shot-put.

I have so many amazing sporting memories. The one that stands out is the 2012 London Paralympics. Though I'm not a paralympian, I was given the once-in-a-lifetime honour of carrying the Paralympic torch. Early that August morning in 2012 we assembled at our set meeting point wearing our white tracksuits. There were five of us and we'd been chosen from the group of blind cricketers that Beth had trained. Three of us were accompanied by guide dogs; Rikki was with me, Thomas with Diane and Jess with Sarah. Each of us had a specific section of the route to cover. Mine was the last stretch, and it could not be more fitting that I had the immense honour and privilege of carrying the torch into Lord's, the home of world cricket. At the end of the day we were offered the opportunity to purchase the torch we had carried. They did not have to ask me twice. The torch is proudly displayed in my living room as a great reminder of the incredible privileges I've enjoyed as a sports enthusiast, and that any dream you can imagine is achievable.

Having the Olympics in London was amazing. I remember being interviewed by a journalist who clearly already had an angle for her story in mind. She wanted to let people know how hard life would be for disabled communities during the Olympics. I don't think my comments impressed her. "I believe London is ready and I, for one, can't wait for the games to come. Londoners have wonderful disability awareness and it's something they can be proud of."

I was right. Rikki was, as usual, excellent at guiding me on the busy underground – in fact, she seemed to thrive on it. We moved faster than any other commuters around. I often heard tourists say, "Follow the girl with the dog, they obviously know the best way."

Chapter 22: A dream come true

Having a successful career has always been very important to me, not only because I am ambitious by nature but because it contributes a great deal towards being independent and fulfilling my passions. The job offer from Guide Dogs ticked all the boxes. I'd be working for an organisation I truly believed in, I'd have the opportunity to grow, and I'd be able to work towards gaining my work permit.

Being on a student visa limited me to working 20 hours a week, and also meant I could not really move up within the organisation. I hardly let this deter me though. I took on extra responsibilities and worked many extra hours to prove my worth. The first few years, working under Nick, Devina and Nikki, went quite well. I developed new fundraising initiatives that had a very good return on investment and could ultimately be run entirely by volunteers.

The first Guide Dog event I organised was one of Nick's initiatives, called Stride for Sight. Teams would consist of up to eight participants. While two team members – one sighted and one blind-folded – walked around an athletics field for 12 hours, the rest of the team would take part in fun, awareness-raising activities on the centre pitch. For whatever reason, there was a lot of office politics surrounding the event, but

Nick was determined to let it go ahead. (I'd only learn of the politics long after the event was over.) Despite obstacles, we raised valuable funds and support for the organisation.

I was very excited when I was given the go-ahead to try out the Jailbreak concept, but its initial reception was a little disappointing. Wherever I went I was met with cautious pessimism and I was never allowed to arrest more than one or two participants. In South Africa, we always arrested between 20 and 30 participants during a Jailbreak event.

We eventually had a breakthrough, though, and the organisation and the Jailbreak concept received some great media coverage. A fellow fundraiser approached the then-conservative politician, Anne Widecombe, who agreed to be arrested, with The Clink Prison Museum as the chosen holding facility. We arrested Anne outside the Houses of Parliament in London and she was taken to "prison" in the back of a police van. The media loved it. Leading up to the event, I had mostly dealt with Anne's PA, who informed me that Anne would raise funds prior to the event and that we could expect an amount of at least £5 000. Sadly, that never materialised. Like a true politician, Anne could not be taken at her word and her inaction very nearly cost my managers and me our jobs. The media coverage was priceless though and the budget for the event was less than £100. Some of my team members stood outside The Clink in the bitter cold asking passers-by to make a donation if they wanted Anne to remain in prison. We made a valuable £300 with this idea. It was a pity we couldn't give the public what they wanted.

Guide Dogs went through a restructure after Nick, Devina and Nikki left. I was given the option of becoming part of the office administration team in fundraising. It was either that or I could choose to leave. It was very frustrating. With my gift of the gab and Rikki by my side, I felt I had the potential to raise lots of funds for the organisation and putting me in an admin role would be a waste. The other female members of the team made the situation a little more bearable, though, and Lynn, Leigh and Dawn helped me through a very tough time in my life.

Once I graduated, I was allowed to obtain a postgraduate visa. This meant I could work full-time for two years in the UK. What bliss! The hunt began for a suitable position. This time, fortunately, I did not have to look far. I became aware of an internal vacancy within the major donor fundraising team of Guide Dogs. I contacted Colette, the manager of the team. After a friendly chat on the phone, we set a date for an interview for later that week. I was asked to prepare a short presentation on how I would approach the role of Major Donor Fundraiser. I had some great ideas. The Paralympics were due in London the following year and most of my presentation was centred on this. I believed it was the perfect opportunity to showcase the independence and confidence that a guide dog could give a visually-impaired person. Maybe my presentation went down well, or maybe Rikki cuddled her way into the hearts of the panel; either way, we got the job.

Being a major donor fundraiser meant that I sourced and looked after high net-worth supporters of the organisation. One such man was Richard Brindle. My predecessor in the role handed this account to me and she did a great job. Together with the London Guide Dogs training team, we designed a proposal for Richard to support their early training project. It resulted in the biggest individual donation made to the organisation at that time. I was also tasked with organising major donor events. The first event we organised was at Dans Les Noir in London, a restaurant where guests eat in complete darkness and are served by blind waiters. Once the three-course meal was completed, the menu was revealed in the lit-up lounge area. The diners' faces were priceless as they realised they had eaten dishes containing shark meat and tripe.

I was back in my groove, doing the job I loved and making a difference while doing so. Colette was a great manager who allowed me to grow and be creative. She also kept an eye on me and made sure that I maintained a healthy work-life balance. Rikki and I travelled a lot for work and we loved it. We met so many interesting people.

One of the other fundraisers we organised was something that I had proposed at my interview. We took current and potential high net-worth donors to some of the heats and finals at the 2012 Paralympics. We ensured that these included visually-impaired participants. My favourite was the evening athletics. Like all other events, it was sold out and the atmosphere was magical. Not only did we watch visually-impaired athletes, we also witnessed some of the greatest paralympians of all time going for gold. We also unknowingly witnessed the blade runner's last race in the national colours of South Africa. It was the final relay and South Africa won gold. I could not have been more proud.

There were so many great events. I just have to share one more: the major donor event at Buckingham Palace in 2013, which Colette organised. Together with current and prospective donors, we would have tea with Princess Anne at the palace.

I was not well at the time but looked forward to the event so much. I remember getting dressed in fancy trousers and a silk blouse. Finding shoes was an issue. The only appropriate shoes I had were the ones I had worn to my brother's wedding seven years earlier. I hated heels but on occasions like these I guess you have to grin and bear it. Travelling in heels on the tube is not recommended. At the event we were all standing so I found no relief there. Rikki, however, treated the palace like her own. They were, of course, expecting her and special copper bowls filled with cool water awaited her at the venue door. The room we used was right behind the balcony where the royals normally stand and wave to the crowds. The wicked side of me so desperately wanted to go out onto the balcony just to see the reaction of the tourists outside the palace. That, of course, was not allowed. What a shame.

Chapter 23: Heartache and loss

As much fun as the event at the palace was, 2013 was actually a very difficult year and I had to deal with quite a few unexpected health issues. I was on my way to see one of our loyal donors, a lovely elderly lady who lived in Kent, when I started experiencing rather severe pain in the most embarrassing place, my bum. Many moons ago I had experienced the same kind of pain when I had haemorrhoids, so assumed that that was the cause of my agony. I held my poise with great difficulty throughout my visit with this lovely lady, but afterwards I begged the cab driver to stop at the nearest chemist. I struggled to see the products on the shelves so finding it on my own would take forever. As with so many times before, this visit to the chemist would mean putting my pride in my pocket and asking for help. Though the assistant was helpful, she was hardly discreet. After I softly and gently explained to her what my problem was, she hollered across the store to the pharmacist: "John! This lady with the guide dog needs some haemorrhoid cream and maybe some suppositories. She has severe anal pain."

Had I not felt so weak from the pain, I would have given her a good talking to regarding customer privacy and using a little discretion.

All this effort and embarrassment was in vain as the meds made no difference to the pain. I made an emergency appointment at the GP who, after having a look, sent me to the hospital. Apparently I had a very big cyst. I had had it for some time but the doctor at the hospital back then said it was nothing. Nothing my ass! At the hospital a young doctor told me he would have to operate the next morning and that I had to be at St Mary's Hospital at 6:30 am. He then gave me a small dose of liquid morphine and sent me home. The morphine made the journey on the bus home more bearable, but by the time I arrived home, the effect had worn off and the pain returned with a vengeance. I called Carol and asked her to please take care of Rikki for the weekend. When she arrived she could see I was not well.

"Tree, are you ok?" she asked.

"I'll be fine, thanks for looking after Rikki."

"Can't I do anything else for you?"

"No, please don't worry, I'm okay."

If only I had accepted her offer.

That was the start of probably the longest night of my life. My pride and stubborn independent streak had gotten the better of me again. The pain was not just back. It actually felt like it was intensifying by the minute. Why I had not just reached out and asked for help is beyond me. I could not sleep. I tried listening to audio books to make the time pass more quickly but whenever I looked at the clock it was as though the minutes were on a go-slow. I tried taking painkillers but only vomited them out within minutes. Even just a small amount of water made me ill. By midnight, I was crawling on the floor, digging my nails into the carpet. When the clock finally came somewhere close to an appropriate hour, I called for a cab. I arrived at the hospital at 6am but the department I needed to go to was closed. Only an unfriendly janitor was there to greet me. When he told me he couldn't help me, my last resolve broke. I slumped into a heap at the door and started to sob uncontrollably. I was not able to stop until I went into theatre later that morning.

Waking up with no pain felt almost heavenly. There also seemed to be a buzz of excitement all around me. At first I thought it was the meds. I later learnt that St Mary's was abuzz, not because my bum felt better, but because Kate and William's firstborn, George had made his arrival just a floor below me.

I was discharged a day later and although the pain was gone, my heart was weighed down with worry. The doctor had informed me that the op was just a temporary solution. I had what was called a complicated anal fistula – a massive abscess with legs like an octopus. The concern was that the legs of this octopus came alarmingly close to other vital organs. I had to return for a far more complicated operation followed by weeks on my tummy in bed. During this op, something simulating a cable tie was planted in my butt. It had to remain there to drain the octopus for several months. This was not only very uncomfortable but meant no sport. No cricket, no sailing, no tennis. For me there was nothing worse.

This is also why I hadn't felt myself at our event at Buckingham Palace. Being inactive for so long meant that I had picked up weight as well. After the event, Colette and I went for drinks with the director of fundraising, Janet. Out of the blue, she blurted: "You've picked up weight, haven't you, Theresa?" I was stunned. Colette was furious. She explained my situation but Janet only nodded. I felt terrible walking home. I knew she was a hard woman, but this time she seemed to have become even more calculating and cold in her treatment of her team members. A little voice inside me said there was more to this, but I put it down to my dip in confidence due to my health, and told the little voice to shut up.

It was also a heart-breaking year for everyone at the Lodge – staff and residents alike. Carl, a friend of Sarah's and mine, suddenly passed away one evening in his sleep. Our friend Dave discovered him. For the next few months, Sarah, Dave and I spent a lot of time together, crying, drinking and even smoking hash. It was hard and the choices I made were not always the best, but it was how we coped with this sudden loss. Dave had many health issues as he had undergone several organ transplants in his life. Like Carl, he was also in his thirties. He seemed to be getting on very well. He had a tube going into his stomach, which he used to take in a healthy amount of water. Dave, being Dave, did not just stick to water. Beer and whiskey also made their way down through the tube. I guess that was not the best thing, but Dave said he could still taste it and, like the hash, it helped a lot with the pain in a way the meds never could. Dave made great progress that year and I even helped him apply for courses to local colleges. One Sunday night later that year, Dave and I had takeaways as usual, but he wasn't himself.

"Dave, let's take you to A&E just to be safe," I said.

"No, I have an appointment first thing tomorrow, I will go then."

"Fine, but I don't have work tomorrow so I will come with you to keep you company. Hospitals can be so boring."

"Cool, mate. That would be great."

With that, we said our goodnights and arranged to meet at 10 the next morning. I couldn't shake my unease and went back to his flat later that night. Dave was in bed and did not look well at all. He wasn't responding coherently to my questions. He did, however, make it clear that he would only go to hospital the next day.

I should have called an ambulance. I shouldn't have waited. But I did.

The next morning, my doorbell rang. It was a staff member asking me to attend a meeting at the office before going to see Dave. I was busy getting dressed and as soon as I was done I went to the office. Paul, the centre coordinator, was there with two paramedics.

"It's Dave, Theresa," said Paul.

"Yes, I know he's not well. We are going to the hospital as soon as he is ready."

"I'm sorry, Theresa, but Dave passed away in his sleep."

I felt my legs give way. One of the paramedics helped me to a chair. "I should have called the ambulance last night, but I didn't. He would have been fine if I'd only listened to my gut." I was so angry with myself.

Dave died of organ failure. I was told that phoning

the ambulance the night before wouldn't have made any difference. I won't ever know and to this day still find it hard to forgive myself.

The year of heartache at the lodge wasn't quite over yet. My neighbour, Tim, also played cricket for the Devils. He would sometimes play music quite loudly but no one minded because we all knew that if he was doing this it meant he was feeling very happy. This was the case one Sunday afternoon, and why it was such a shock to see the police at his flat the next day.

"Is Tim okay?" I asked the officer at his door. "I'm not at liberty to say."

I rushed to the office. Tim had died the night before. I believe it was from a heart attack.

Losing three friends in their thirties was devastating, but 2013 still had one more blow in store …

Chapter 24: Breaking point

Our major donor team was growing with new staff members coming on board. We had all been invited to a venue in London, together with Richard, the CEO of Guide Dogs. The purpose of the meeting was to gauge the potential of the venue as an option for hosting a new major donor event. I had a great amount of respect for Richard, but on this day, every other senior staff member present seemed unusually cold and stand-offish and hardly spoke a word to us. I was not the only one who picked up on this and the rest of the team related the same feeling over lunch.

Two weeks later, we had our monthly team meeting with Colette. Just as we were about to start, Tracey, Colette's manager and two HR representatives entered the room. Tracey unceremoniously took over from Colette. She conveyed the shocking news that the whole team were being made redundant and that only one major donor fundraiser would remain. Volunteers would, from then on, do the work. I had so many questions but the shock was so intense that I found it hard to talk sense.

Earlier that year, Guide Dogs had implemented a system where staff could be evaluated based on the contribution they made to the organisation. It protected the organisation if a staff member did not deliver, but it also helped employees to know whether they were on track. Should an employee not meet targets, managers would have an opportunity to communicate this to them and put remedial action in place to improve the situation. In our case, this was never done. During the meeting, I asked Tracey if the decision would have been the same if we had brought in more funds for the organisation. She could not answer.

Colette, as our manager, had also been kept in the dark. It was never communicated to her that this kind of action was on the cards. My heart went out to our newest members. Some had only been with us for three months and a few had relocated to be able to join the team. During the shocker of a meeting, I managed to ask Tracey if they were still considering an application for a work permit for me. The research into whether this was possible had already been done and Colette had sent the proposal to Tracey earlier in the year.

"I'm not sure what you're talking about," said Tracey nervously.

"Yes you do," said Colette. "We have spoken about this on several occasions and you have all the information on paper."

My chair was close to where Tracey sat. I looked at her and, with a pleading, desperate voice asked, "Did you take this into consideration when making this decision?"

Tracey made eye contact with one of the HR representatives then turned back to me and said: " You can apply for the full-time role just like anyone else."

"But for that I'd need the work permit application too."

"I'll have to get back to you on that but I don't think we can do it."

I was filled with so much anger, heartache, disappointment and resentment. I had been working for Guide Dogs for seven years and had given everything I possibly could. I was within reach of the ultimate prize: a work permit that would eventually result in permission to remain in the UK indefinitely. In my book, this would be the manifestation of the independence I had been working towards for so many years.

After the meeting, we all slumped off to the nearest pub. Not even my favourite G&T helped. I felt so betrayed. Guide Dogs was not a perfect organisation and working for them was not always easy. With the exception of a handful of individuals, the staff were not ready to accommodate a team member with a visual impairment. It was a challenge to get documents in an accessible format and to have meeting presentations made available electronically. I even had a major battle on my hands when I tried to persuade them not to state that a driver's licence was essential when advertising vacancies. This automatically excluded any visually-impaired applicants. For me, one of the most difficult things to comprehend was the inaccessibility of the organisation's head office in Reading. It was not in town and buses did not go past there often. The bus stop was quite a distance away from the entrance and, for me, very dangerous. It was not well-lit and could leave someone like me in a very vulnerable position with no help or hope of assistance within reach, should it ever be required. The entrance itself was just as poorly lit, which made accessing the front door at reception unnecessarily difficult, especially in winter.

None of these issues ever stopped me from loving the organisation that I worked for or from passionately promoting the work that we did.

After the initial shock, I pulled myself together and started looking at alternative opportunities within the organisation. Two came up – one in a different fundraising department called Name a Puppy, and the other in the volunteering department. I called the manager of Name a Puppy first. I knew her well because our departments had often worked together. She sounded quite shocked that I wanted to apply. "It involves computer work," she said.

"I am aware of that, but I am quite good at using a computer, thanks to the relevant accessible software."

"Well, I don't think it would be for you. I don't think you will cope with the work with your eye condition."

I was stunned. Again.

The other vacancy was within another department that I knew quite well: volunteering. During this interview, someone entered the room, spoke to the panel and walked out. I later learnt it was the head of the department.

"Was someone in the room just now?" I asked.

"Yes," replied the representative.

"That does not make sense. We all know it is basic manners to let a visually-impaired person know when someone enters the room and when they leave."

I was met with an uncomfortable silence. Though I was more than qualified, I did not get the job. I was the only internal and visually-impaired candidate. By the organisation's very own standards, this should have increased my prospects tenfold. They never did say why my application was unsuccessful.

Chapter 25: The last straw

I was in a very dark place, and not for the first time in my life. There was one more blow that finally caused me to crash. Rikki was such a fantastic guide dog. She had a very high workload and we travelled quite a bit for work, sport and leisure. She even became a favourite on the Soho club scene. She always gave the doorman or lady that irresistible look that got us in free. But the fact that she had such a high workload, also meant that she had to retire early. She started slowing down a bit in the summer of 2013 and, after she was assessed by Guide Dogs, it was decided in September of that year that she was to retire.

Although it was absolutely the right decision, it could not have happened at a worse time in my life. It felt like she was just about the only thing I still had going for me. Rikki was adopted by a lovely family who live on a small farm in Kent. The set up was heaven for her with lots of animals, kids and, best of all, a pool. She even made friends with the cats. I was happy that she had found a new mum in Linda, who loved her very much. We are still in contact to this day. But losing Rikki left a massive, gaping hole in my heart and robbed me of a lot of joy.

The evening before my final meeting with Guide Dogs I sat completely alone in my flat. I was to meet with Tracey and the

HR representatives the next day. I had so many questions but I knew no matter what I asked, the situation would remain the same. I should have reached out for help. I opted instead for the final curtain, not for the first time in my life.

Even though the sexual assault in 2007 had set in motion a series of events that ultimately changed my life for the better, it actually took quite a devastating toll on my emotional health and wellbeing. Instead of dealing with the trauma, I buried myself in my work. This is something I had always done. For the second time in my life, my body cried out and crashed. I found myself planning my suicide down to the finest detail. I would jump in front of a tube. I came so close. One evening, standing on an overhead bridge at a small station called Stamford Brook, I was busy timing when to jump. My timing had to be perfect. I could not fall too soon, lest the driver would stop, and I could not jump too late and miss the train. A little voice told me to give life one more chance. I phoned the crisis line. I said where I was and how I felt. The man on the other end of the line told me I could not be admitted as there weren't any beds available. I pleaded. I needed help. How could he just leave me like this? I was incredibly upset with him. He told me my life was not in danger. He told me I was probably just upset because I wasn't getting my way. I put the phone down. I was fuming, and that was the last straw.

Just as I was about to climb over the barrier of the bridge, my phone rang. It was Nikki. How did she know? We had a long talk and she convinced me to go home and see my doctor the next day. He had me admitted to a mental health unit. The mental health care system in the UK is so very different from that of South Africa. You share facilities with patients who could be deemed dangerous. One nearly attacked me with a knife for no reason. Guide dogs aren't allowed in these establishments, not even for visits. It's a strange policy, as being separated from your four-legged partner only increases any stress and loneliness of a visually-impaired patient tenfold. The system is also ill-equipped in accommodating visually-impaired patients, and the forms are not accessible. I was put in a room with no curtains. At night one of the patients would bang on my door and scream profanities at me. When I asked if this could be stopped, I was told to rather be more accommodating of other patients. Then the hospital's heating broke down and we were given the option to receive home care. They did not have to ask me twice.

A follow-up appointment was made for me at the Ilford Mental Health Centre. I arrived full of hope with Rikki my new guide dog at my side. I waited at reception. My doctor, an Indian woman, came down the stairs. She did not greet me but pointed at Rikki and asked, "What's that?"

"It's my guide dog, Rikki," I said with a smile. She said nothing and I followed her upstairs.

"May I please sit with my back to the window?" I asked. "I struggle with the light in my eyes."

"No," she said abruptly. "That is my seat."

By this time I was very uncomfortable as Rikki and I were obviously not welcome. She opened my file. "Oh, so you really can't see?"

"Yes ma'am, that's why I have Rikki to help me."

Then I did the unthinkable and asked, “Is this the first time you are looking at my notes? Should you not have done some preparation?”

She took my file and left the room. She came back, told me I was bipolar and then left without greeting or giving any advice.

I was gutted and walked home sobbing. I was put on medication that made me feel like I had lost half of my personality. Only once I moved and fell under a new healthcare department were my needs met. I did go back to the Ilford Mental Health Centre and spoke to the man in charge.

“I believe one of two things, possibly both, happened,” I explained. “My doctor did not prepare for my visit. She was not at all trained in the field of disability awareness.”

His reply, “I can’t comment on that,” was all I got, not even an apology.

About two years after this incident, in 2009, I found myself in a dark place again. Nikki had moved back to Scotland and, due to the restructuring at Guide Dogs, my job responsibilities had changed. Our new office manager, Louis, was probably the worst manager I have ever had to work for. Though I hadn’t realised it at the time, Louis took complete advantage of me and abused the situation I was in. He knew full well I would do anything for Guide Dogs and for my career. He overloaded me with added responsibilities that all had to be done in secret. I became alienated from the team and was heading for a breakdown. To compound my situation even further, I was also living with two female housemates from hell.

It was a Friday morning when I woke up feeling physically

and emotionally unwell. I managed to get an emergency appointment with a GP who prescribed strong calming tablets. Later that morning while sitting at my desk, I took one tablet. No result. I took another. By the time I eventually did start to feel any kind of effect, I had already taken four. The packet contained only eight. It was then that the deep, dark thoughts came back. It would be so much easier if I could go to sleep and never wake up. I took the rest of the tablets. Rikki was lying on her bed next to me. I decided to sit with her and give her a cuddle. I closed my eyes and disappeared into a world of blissful nothingness. I heard voices but I could not respond. I woke up in hospital the next day: it had not worked. I was both relieved and terrified at the same time. I was admitted to a different mental health unit this time. It felt safe and the aftercare service was good. It was this mental health team that helped me to get accommodation at the lodge and for things to change at work. Louis was asked to leave.

Now, four years later and for a third time, I found myself wrestling with those same dark thoughts I had come to know so well. I had a considerable amount of sleeping tablets and decided to take them all. I did not want to wake up. Not ever. After I had swallowed them, a little voice started nagging me to phone for help. I did, and I don't remember much after that.

I woke up in a hospital in the early hours of the morning. I was completely drugged up and often not sure where I was or even who I was. A few hours later, someone approached me. I was in such a daze I could not tell if the person was black or white, male or female.

"You know where the psychiatry department is? Just down the street."

I could hardly respond.

"You can make your own way there, they are expecting you."

I remember getting up and asking for directions. With help from strangers, I finally made it there. Still totally spaced out, I heard the receptionist telling me to take a seat. I then noticed the needle of a drip in the back of my hand. The hospital staff had forgotten to remove it. The receptionist saw it too.

"Why do you still have that on you?" I struggled to respond.

"I will get someone to look at it. But no one can see you right now, so you will just have to sit here and wait."

And so I did. Out of nowhere, I suddenly remembered the meeting with Tracey and the two representatives from HR. I asked for the time and realised I would be late if I wanted to go. The needle in my hand really bugged me. I went to the toilet and promptly ripped it out. I was a little shocked by the amount of blood that could come from such a small hole. I managed to control it by covering it with toilet paper.

When I got back to my chair, the receptionist realised what I had done and was furious.

"What did you do? Where is the needle? This place is full of drug addicts just waiting to use it. You really should think of others too you know."

I sat back in my chair after my scolding. Memories of previous mental hospitals I had been admitted to came flooding back. If I stayed here, I would be heading for the same hell. I stood up and left.

The receptionist either did not see me or she simply did not care. Either way, no one ever came looking for me or even called to ask if was okay. I didn't even go home. I called my client representative, Chris, and told him I was on my way but would be late.

Chris worked in the events team and I knew him well. He met me at Euston Station and knew immediately that something was very wrong. I told him I had just come from the hospital and was feeling drowsy. I wanted to get the meeting over and done with. I did not tell him everything. We made our way back to the office where the first awful meeting had taken place.

I wondered if they noticed the state I was in, drowsy from the overdose, white as a sheet, shaking, eyes bloodshot and still in the scraggy clothes from the day before. If they did, it did not matter to them. It was so hard to talk sense and I cannot even remember much of their responses. Most of the time though, Tracey came back with: "You can always apply for the one remaining role, everyone is entitled to do that."

Not me. My postgraduate visa came to an end that month and there were only two options: a work permit or continuing with my studies and going back on a student visa. Tracey made it clear in the first meeting that a work permit was not an option. Being on a student visa meant I could apply only for a part-time role of 20 hours a week. I asked if they would consider this. Another "no" shattered my last hopes.

I went back to my lonely flat and then decided to let go of my stubborn pride. I called Colette, opened my heart and told her everything including the overdose, walking out of the hospital and, of course, the terrible meeting with Tracey. She was there within minutes. We went back to her flat and I felt safe even if it was just for those few days.

Colette is very talented and could find work very easily. Her heart, however, was not in London. She yearned for a different lifestyle. Unlike most people, her dream was not just a mere fantasy. A year later, she packed all her belongings into her little car and with her pooch Jampa in tow, moved to a small town near Malaga close to the sunny Spanish coast. She's never looked back. I have such great respect and admiration for people who take bold steps to get to where they want to be.

By the end of 2013 my life had come to a junction. Do I stay and study? Or do I go? Staying on a student visa would mean going back to living in a room in a shared house. The mere thought of having to find a decent place to live and the almost impossible task of getting housemates who were bearable filled me with absolute dread. I could study only for a doctorate since anything less would not get me to the 10-year mark living in the UK, which is what I needed for the option of permanent residency. I'd also have to find new employment but wouldn't be able to get anything where they could offer me anything more than an entry-level salary. Going would mean leaving the UK and returning to South Africa permanently only to face a life of very limited independence.

I knew I'd never be able to make this decision on my own. Not in my current state. I needed guidance and advice. I immediately thought of my uncle Charl. After a chat on the phone, I booked a ticket to South Africa to visit my uncle for a week or two. During my visit, Charl never made my choice for me. He gave me great advice and offered me a listening ear.

Throughout my visit, a little voice kept on saying: “Maybe this is where you belong.”

“But how? You know you’re lost in this place if you can’t drive,” I reprimanded the annoying little voice.

I spoke to Charl and heard myself saying to him, “Uncle Charl, I want to come back. I have no idea how I am going to make it here, but my gut feeling says the same thing day and night.”

The next day Charl came back to me with a job offer.

“I needed to hear you say that you wanted to come back, before I could make you the offer.”

I flew back to London the next day to pack the rest of my belongings and say my goodbyes. By the end of December I was back in my home country, excited and terrified all at once.

Chapter 26: A third miracle brings new light

Being back in South Africa was every bit the shock to my system I had expected it to be. For the first month I stayed with my parents in Nelspruit. I had been there for about a week before I ventured out to the local grocery store for the first time. The security guard stopped me.

"What is that?" he asked pointing to my white cane.

"It is my cane sir."

"No, it's not allowed!" he said sternly.

"I'm blind sir and this cane helps me," I tried to explain.

"No, you're not allowed with that thing."

My patience was running out.

"Sir, I believe you are wrong. Here's an idea – go to the manager and ask him. If he says I must leave, I promise I will leave."

With that, I ignored his objections and went ahead and did my shopping. The manager later apologised, but this incident confirmed that being back home was going to be a bumpy ride.

As soon as I arrived in South Africa, I applied to South African

Guide Dogs for a new guide dog. I waited 12 months before I was finally matched and invited to attend training at their centre in Johannesburg. This was where I had been for training with Sandy, my first guide dog.

There were five of us in the class, Jean-Marie, a student from North West, Ilze, a school-leaver from Tzaneen, and John and Frieda, a married couple from the Northern Cape. Everyone was there for their first guide dog except me. The married couple was an interesting pair. John was a preacher and Frieda his devoted wife. John could not stop talking politics on the long bus rides and Frieda constantly sang gospel songs to herself, not talking to anyone. I escaped both by putting on my headphones and soon the other classmates followed suit.

John believed that nothing from the Western world should ever have come to Africa and only caused problems.

"That's interesting, John," I said. "Do you mean no roads or electricity or anything like that?"

"Yes," he replied boldly.

"We were happy just herding cattle and then the colonisers came along," he muttered.

"What about your guide dog, John?"

"What do you mean what about my guide dog?"

"South African Guide Dogs, as we were informed at the induction, was started by Gladys Evans from the UK. Hence the centre was named after her. There are now many other countries that have guide dog schools, but I believe it all started in Europe. If you don't want anything from any of these countries it should include your guide dog, right?"

I was met with silence and John muttered something to his wife. The trainers later called me in and asked that I not cause any more upset in the class.

John, however controversial his opinions might have been, was a great guide-dog owner. He looked after Keely very well and they made a great team. Frieda, on the other hand, had us all worried. As soon as the instructors turned their backs, she would break all the rules. One such occasion was when we took our dogs to spend. For those who don't know, this means pooh time. Frieda was matched with a beautiful black Labrador called Jewel. After feeding our dogs at five in the afternoon, we would take them on their leads to spend. This is very important training. It is crucial that your dog feels comfortable spending on the lead when you ask it to. They get trained to do so from a young age and then it is our responsibility to keep it up. It could take anything from five to 30 minutes. Patience is key and Frieda seemed to be in short supply when it came to Jewel's spending. She gave Jewel only five minutes before putting her back in her pen and returning to her own room. An hour later, we would retrieve our dogs from the pens to join us at the dinner table. This was an opportunity to see how they behaved while their owners enjoyed their meal.

Frieda loved dressing up. This particular evening she wore a pretty white dress and sparkly bling sandals. Jewel, not having had enough time to relieve herself earlier, had left a lovely present for Frieda in the spending area of her pen, which was right next to ours. I had a front-row seat view of what was about to unfold. Frieda hadn't seen the gift Jewel had left her and was ignoring our cautions from the sideline. Jewel's parcel of pooh resembled perfectly scooped balls of ice cream and I could tell it was still rather new. Frieda stepped right into the middle of it, steaming fresh piles of pooh, squishing through her toes and covering her once-sparkly sandal. I took my dog and ran to my room. I would have been in so much trouble had I burst out laughing within earshot of Madam No-More-Sparkles. I reached my room just in time. I nearly wet myself, rolling on the floor with laughter. As karmic penance I've stepped in several parcels myself since then, but I still have a good laugh just thinking about Frieda's folly. The trainers eventually removed Jewel from her and matched her with someone who treated her with the love and care she deserved.

Ilze was from Tzaneen, a small farming community in South Africa's North. Her story still sends shivers down my spine. She had been in a terrible accident in her final school year. A drunk driver had crashed into her car, killing her friend and himself. Ilze was left seriously injured and fighting for her life. She spent the next year in high care. Her face and leg were reconstructed and her injuries left her with minimal sight. Despite the trauma she had been through, she was still such a positive person. She had every reason to be angry and resentful but she was quite the opposite. She was positive about her future and did not hold on to her past.

Our trainers in class were Karen and Permit. On day two, Permit announced the plans for the evening:

"Tonight, and every night, we will have pap at six."

"Really? Pap every night?" I replied in despair.

"Yes, I thought you would like that."

I love pap. It's a local maize meal porridge, a very economical dish and a staple for many of the poorer families in South Africa. Usually served for breakfast, it is also served with a tomato and onion relish as a side dish at a barbecue. I could appreciate that this was a charity organisation and that they'd try to keep costs down. But pap every night?

Karen saw the look of disbelief on my face.

"Theresa, he means pub, not pap."

"Oh pub!" I exclaimed. "Thank God for that!"

I was matched with Kelsey, the sister of John's Keely and Kwezi, who was Ilze's dog. They were all beautiful white Labradors, and Kelsey took first prize at being mischievous. She was much bigger than Sandy and Rikki, something I had to get used to. Though she might have been quite naughty off lead, she was a brilliant dog to train with. It was hard at first because every time I looked at her, I'd be reminded of Rikki and it made my heart hurt. The training was slightly different from that in the UK, but the results were the same: a miracle on four legs.

While training with our dogs, our class was invited to a show in aid of South African Guide Dogs. Des and Dawn, a well-known husband-and-wife duo in South Africa who sing folk music, performed that night. They held a special place in our family as they had performed at an event where the family business won the "Franchisor of the Year" award. At the Guide Dog function I asked to be introduced to them and it was arranged. We had only a quick chat, but it was really special to be able to record a message with them and send it to my uncle.

Three years later, I bumped into them again. I was nominated for the Margaret Hirsch "Women in Business" award and attended a glamorous gala at Montecasino in Johannesburg. To match the theme of the event, "An Enchanted Forest", the usual 'red carpet' was in fact green. Poor Kelsey thought it was perfect ... While we were posing for a photo with Margaret Hirsch, Kelsey relieved herself on what must have looked like grass. I pretended not to see a thing and quickly moved on.

Dawn was the keynote speaker at the event. She was really incredibly inspirational and I asked to meet her again. I couldn't believe that she remembered me. Then Kelsey made sure that she would absolutely never forget us. She emptied her bladder on the bottom of Dawn's ball gown, leaving it soaking wet. I was really embarrassed but also worried. Kelsey had never done this before and she had been out spending just before we entered the venue. I later learnt that a well-meaning waiter had given her a huge bowl of water under the table. That night certainly was one to remember, as I also won an award. Nevertheless, I do hope Dawn's dry-cleaning bill was not too high. Fortunately, I know she loves dogs.

Chapter 27: A successful new career

The job my uncle offered me was at his company: The Success Academy. They build office parks and then let the space to other businesses. The philosophy of the company is to create, and provide their tenants with, an environment in which they will be able to succeed.

Overseeing the company's corporate social responsibility (CSR) projects was part of my job description. One of these was Save our Planet, Plant a Tree. The aim of the project was to donate 150 000 trees to the local community. We did this by approaching one school a month, where we would give each pupil a two-year-old indigenous tree to take care of and plant at home. I was responsible for arranging and hosting the tree ceremonies at each school. I absolutely loved it.

Talking to the children and getting them excited about the environment was more fulfilling than I ever imagined it could be. I explained to them that superheroes are not just fictional characters, and that anyone who could save a life was a superhero. They always agreed with me on this point. I'd then go on to explain that trees give oxygen, which keeps us alive. If they were to plant trees they, too, would save lives and so also deserve the title of superhero. They loved this.

I also assisted with arranging networking events for our tenants and local businesses. Charl offered a training programme for his tenants called "The Servant Philosophy", sharing the business knowledge he had gained over 40 years. The principle of his teaching is based on his theory that money, like water, flows down and not up. To receive money, you need to act in service of others. Charl, for example, serves his tenants and is a landlord in a class of his own. He does not just collect rent at the end of the month – he takes a sincere interest in the wellbeing, success and growth of his tenants.

Becoming part of The Success Academy team was much easier than I expected. Experience had made me wary that not all people and not all employers adjust well to having a staff member with a disability on board. All the necessary adjustments were put in place from the start. The right IT equipment was procured and I even had a driver. No longer did I need to concern myself with people doubting my ability. The only thing I needed to prove was that I had acquired the job on merit and not because I was family.

Charl was a firm believer in self-development and would support his staff in their endeavours to do so. We spoke at length about my studies and he encouraged me not to close this chapter of my life. With his motivation and assistance I applied to study for my master's qualification.

Chapter 28: A master mind

Distance learning in South Africa is a challenge at the best of times. Doing so when you have special needs that include visual impairment aids can become a nightmare. The University of South Africa (UNISA) is the main port of call if you wish to follow this route for postgraduate studies. While UNISA claim to have a department dedicated to looking after the needs of visually-impaired students, they have a poor reputation for supplying study material in general, never mind in an accessible format. I struggled for six whole months to get the relevant information from them and eventually just gave up.

My search for an institution that would be able to support my needs took me back to the UK. I learnt that it would be possible to obtain my masters online, with tutoring via Skype. The University of Chester ticked all the right boxes; they were ready to support me and came highly recommended. I gathered all the necessary info from them and submitted a proposal to my uncle. The University of Chester's fees were much higher than UNISA's, but the quality and standard of education simply wasn't comparable. I was worried that the cost might negatively influence the outcome of my proposal, but was pleasantly surprised when Charl gave me the go-ahead. The conditions were the same as they would be for any other member of staff. The knowledge I gained had to benefit the company and shine through in my performance. Should I fail, I would have to repay every cent.

It was daunting but I was up for the challenge. My degree formed part of the university's Work-Based Integrated Studies (WBIS) programme. This meant that my line of study had to be approved by my employer and that my thesis had to be based on a project directly linked to my current job. I decided to do my masters in project design and leadership. Masters come with lots of projects, parts, subjects, guidelines and specifications, the details of which might make your eyes go squint. The main elements, however, included four major sections. First, a self-reflective module had to be studied. The philosophy of the programme was based on experiential learning and your ability to self-reflect. The second project allowed you to stake an Accreditation of Prior Learning (APL) claim for work-related learning that took place in the last five years. This could count for up to 80 credits. Thirdly, I'd have to submit a research proposal and then, finally, the actual thesis or work-based research project.

Completing the self-reflecting project was a wonderful journey in itself. I referred back to a period at Guide Dogs when Louis, my manager at the time, had bullied me into taking on way too much work. Upon self-reflection, I realised that I was so focused on my goal of gaining a work permit that I became a very soft target for the treatment I had to endure. Louis was in the wrong, but the entire episode could have been avoided if I had been more self-aware and had a better work-life balance.

The APL project I chose was a huge endeavour and my tutor, Denise, advised me to put in a claim for the full 80 credits. Guess what it was based upon: Jailbreak! When I left Guide

Dogs UK, I thought that that was the end of Jailbreak. It was not. Years of perfecting and diversifying this project finally paid off. At Guide Dogs UK, I was asked to write a blueprint for the concept. It took months and I wondered if anyone would ever use it. Fortunately, I kept a copy of this document as well as video footage and press clippings of some of the Jailbreak projects we hosted. All of these formed part of my APL claim.

The third part of my masters was to submit a 'Designing Practitioner Research Proposal'. This was a forerunner of the actual project describing, in a nutshell, what my research project would be about and how I would go about doing it. Sounds simple? It was not. My research project was based on the Save our Planet, Plant a Tree project which I had managed for The Success Academy. For this part, I had a different tutor and he was nothing like Denise at all.

Denise was my main tutor throughout my Masters journey except for this part. What an incredible instructor. I excelled under her mentorship and my visual impairment was never an issue for her. She was very supportive and made me believe in my abilities and myself again. It was very different and refreshing in comparison to prior experiences with educators.

Jim was my tutor while I prepared my designing practitioner research proposal. The aim of the project was to assist the company in finding ways to promote the project better and explore the possibility of including it in their brand strategy. Jim had other plans. He had a scientific background and wanted me to concentrate on the environmental impact of the project. It was like pulling teeth. Thank God, Denise was my mentor for the final part of my masters, the actual research project.

When I started the project, it was like a huge mountain to climb – another unknown path for me to travel. Thanks to Denise, I was able to focus on my abilities instead of my disability. I have gained excellent interviewing skills over time and this came in very handy. In July 2017 I received my final mark. I had not only passed, I had passed quite well. Who would have thought the girl with the "sorting gene problem" and who was apparently unable to even climb a set of stairs, would smash a master's degree in project leadership and design?

Chapter 29: A toast

"Fanie de Villiers will be the speaker at our executive breakfast next week," Charl announced one afternoon during a team meeting.

"Vinnige Fanie!" I shouted in amazement and delight. (This was his nickname among his Afrikaans-speaking fans, meaning Fast Fanie.) The rest of the team, bar one or two who understood my excitement, gave me puzzled looks.

"He used to be one of the country's best cricketers and is now a very successful businessman," Charl explained.

I had met Fanie very briefly once before at a blind cricket event. I never considered that he'd remember me, but he did and that fact alone blew my mind. It was hard not to go into total annoying-fan mode. At the end of the event he signed my blind-cricket ball. That in itself was really special, but what proved to have a far greater impact on my life that day was the advice he gave during his presentation.

"If you want to better yourself and if you want to become a world-class leader, join Toastmasters," he said. I was already familiar with Toastmasters, as the judges at the public speaking competitions at school events were usually all members. Toastmasters, in a nutshell, is a non-profit educational organisation that operates clubs worldwide with the aim of helping members improve their communication, public speaking and leadership skills. I had been meaning to join for quite some time but somehow just never got round to it. The next day, after the breakfast, I went online to find my nearest club. There were a couple, but Centurion Toastmasters was perfect because of its proximity and their meeting times. I was excited. Why not? I loved public speaking and if Vinnige Fanie said it was a good idea, I simply could not go wrong.

During the first few meetings I was a quiet observer and did not say much. I probably would have tried hiding in a corner but having Kelsey with me made that impossible. During a meeting in August they finally had my full attention when they made the following announcement:

"The Humorous Speech Contest will take place in September. All members are eligible to participate."

I'd never done this before but it sounded like fun. On the night of the competition my speech went down very well and I desperately wanted to win. I came second, though, and was most annoyed to have been beaten by a man called Dave Caines. Who was he anyway, and how did I not come first? I later learnt that Dave Caines was in fact one of the top, if not the best, humorous speakers in South Africa. He became a mentor and a good friend. Centurion Toastmasters turned out to be rich with talent and had amazing members. I made an effort to spend time with them. Even when I needed a ride, I would ask a member whose brains I could pick while we travelled.

One of the most rewarding parts of Toastmasters is the evaluation of the speakers. Every speech you make is evaluated and you receive invaluable feedback during these sessions. I'll never forget my first evaluation:

"Theresa," said Trevor, my evaluator. "One point you can work on is to look out for hand clasping."

"Hand clasping? I don't do hand clasping, do I? I thought my gestures were the business." Luckily I wasn't thinking out loud (not this time). I decided to look at a recording of my speech. What a shock! There I was indeed – arms pointing straight down, hands clasping and fingers stuck together like cold spaghetti. I looked like an old-fashioned choirgirl. Breaking this habit has required quite some focus and determination.

Listening to and then evaluating fellow speakers was another great way to learn from Toastmasters. Many people assume that listening skills come more readily to people who are visually impaired. Apparently having one disability enhances all your other senses. I don't believe in this theory at all. My loss of sight has increased only my sense of humour. I do, however, use my ears more than my eyes. My eyes were demoted years ago. Like your memory, the more you use your ability to listen the more it improves. And as it turns out, I'm not a half-bad evaluator either. I made it to the finals of one of our national competitions and eventually came third.

Toastmasters have several projects where they give back to the community. One such project is called Speech Craft, a programme designed to help school children gain confidence and skills in public speaking. I like the idea of giving back and offered my assistance. I wasn't sure I'd be of much use as

I'd never really worked with children before. My first Speech Craft project was at a well-known school in Pretoria. The group consisted of about 25 grade eight pupils. I was asked to give a demonstration speech. As many of my talks do, this speech contained a lot of humour. The kids and I had become well acquainted and they knew all about me and Kelsey and why she had to accompany me to each session. I was surprised to see them hanging onto my every word. At the end of my speech, which was all about how karma can be such a cow, I said: "I might have only three per cent sight, but watch out world, I also have 97 per cent attitude."

The following week the students had to present their own speeches. A young, dark-haired boy who looked smaller in stature than all the other boys, confidently walked to the front of the room. He proceeded to give a three-minute talk that would stay with me for life.

The lad had Attention Deficit Disorder (ADD) but instead of hiding it, he used humour to splash it out in the open and, as a result, educate his friends and gain their respect. He had his peers in stitches and me in tears.

That evening after class, when his mum came to pick him up, he grabbed her by the arm, dragged her excitedly over to me and said, "Mum, this is the lady I told you about, the one with three per cent sight and 97 per cent attitude." Leaving his mum stranded with me, he dashed off to greet his friends.

"I don't think you realise what an impact you've had on my boy. He's never spoken openly about his ADD but now he is almost proud of it. Thank you."

Chapter 30: Home alone

I had always wanted to own my own home. Becoming a homeowner is probably one of the best and worst experiences life has to offer. Owning your own home is an amazing feeling. But what you have to go through to get there can be an absolute nightmare.

I imagined that the expense would be my biggest worry, but it paled in comparison to all the other troubles that awaited. The process of finding a home starts relatively easily. You scan the market to see what's available. I remember my parents doing this years ago by going to show houses on weekends. Fortunately we now have the Internet and I could browse online for my dream home. The next part is when the real challenge starts: contacting the agent.

As I was about to make one of the most important decisions of my life and spend a considerable sum of money doing so, I expected a certain level of professionalism. But I quickly learnt that estate agents are a breed of their own. The first agent I phoned answered in a very disgruntled tone. It was 8:30 on a Tuesday morning.

"I am still in my pyjamas," she said, without a hint of shame or remorse. "You can call me back later."

The second agent was refreshingly ready and willing to help. She had a strong Afrikaans accent and struggled with English so I switched to Afrikaans. But she insisted on speaking the English "taal" (language) very deliciously. We arranged to meet at a house I was interested in. When she stepped out of her a beautiful Mercedes Benz, I nearly fainted in horror. She was wearing a leopard-print miniskirt that was so short it left hardly anything to the imagination.

My dream-home requirements, which I had communicated to her, were quite clear and I was not asking for much, I felt. I simply wanted a home that was safe, well looked after and had lots of natural light. Her hearing must have been equal to my sight. She took me to a house that could (or might) have been the perfect drug den. The windows were painted and sealed, and a smell of weed hung in the air. The little garden was so overgrown and neglected that I nearly lost Kelsey in it.

So it went for months. Several agents and several pending disasters later, I finally found an agent who listened to what I wanted, comprehended what I said and took me to a home that was everything I asked for. She took only half an hour of my time and we had hit the jackpot.

Being a homeowner came with another set of challenges. I did not realise these challenges would be multiplied by my visual impairment. Much like my experience with estate agents, my contact with handymen and electricians proved to be a bumpy ride. My first nightmare was finding a reliable electrician. A few things in my new home needed fixing and I knew they weren't going to come cheap. After an arduous search I finally found Jacques, who seemed like a pretty decent bloke and a very capable electrician. He actually seemed such a nice chap that after he had completed what I had hired him to do, I felt I could ask him a small favour. I needed a light bulb to be changed – simple enough for the average person, but I wasn't quite average and I also came with an unfortunate history when it came to all things electrical. It was not dissimilar to my history with driving…

At the age of 14, like most teenagers, I had a slight obsession with music. Wherever I went, so did my boombox, even to the bathroom. My dad indulged my obsession by extending the cord of my radio. One Saturday evening, while I was soaking in the tub, the music stopped. (Horror!) I got out of the bath, wrapped a towel around myself and started to assess the situation. The lead had broken where my dad had made the extension. My family was watching TV.

"I can fix this," I thought to myself. Still just wrapped in the towel, I snuck out to the garage and nicked some of my dad's trusty insulation tape. My basic knowledge of electricity would carry me through this task. I noticed that the electric lead consisted of two lines running parallel: I therefore had four ends staring at me. "All you need is for the line to be solid and it will work," I said to myself out loud. I wove the four ends together and covered them with insulation tape. With one hand clutching the towel, I reached down to the wall socket to switch it on.

BOOOM! Sans towel I flew across my small bedroom and landed on the bed. The power in the house had tripped so the room was dark and filled with smoke. My parents and brothers came rushing down the hall. With a very delayed reaction, I finally managed to utter a pathetic scream. "Eeeehh!"

Torches in hand, my family entered my room. I was okay but in shock and, as a result, could not move. I lay, exposed and embarrassed, on my bed being closely assessed by torchlight. Once it was discovered that I had come to no serious harm, my brothers burst out laughing. My dad made me promise never ever again to attempt any job remotely related to electricity.

This promise and, of course, the experience, resulted in me always asking for assistance, even with something as seemingly simple as changing a light bulb. Jacques was more than happy to help. I was already paying him a considerable amount of money for all the other work in the house, so I assumed this would be considered a small favour. His final bill came as quite a shock.

Item 4 - Changing of a light bulb: R250

Jacques wasn't the only tradesman who tried to chance it and was out to make an easy buck. I had a fair share of so-called handymen who either tried overcharging me or delivered sub-standard work. I believe many of them operated under the assumption that because I was technically blind, I wouldn't be able to see that they'd done only half of the work required or that I would not know any better if they overcharged me for simple jobs. I very quickly learnt that in these situations a hunger for independence would come at a very high financial cost. For once, sense prevailed and I sought advice and support wherever I could.

Chapter 31: Blind cricket in South Africa

I think by now it should be considered a well-established fact that I love my sport. The trip to Nepal had inspired me to such an extent that I decided to start the first all-female blind cricket team in South Africa. My intentions were pure but my ideas were not received with open arms. I wanted things to happen and I wanted them to happen fast. It does not work that way in South Africa. Before I'd even had any proper meetings with Blind Cricket South Africa, I had put arrangements in place for our first game. This left many people within the blind cricket community a little disgruntled and hot under the collar, but in retrospect I can understand why.

Nevertheless, we did get a team together and we played a match against The Titans, the sighted provincial women's team. It was a tremendous day – a day to remember. It received plenty of media attention and was a great experience for all the players involved.

While we were fielding, one of my B1 players who had no sight, went down on her knees, feeling with her hands on the grass all around.

"Mashooda!" I shouted. We've got the ball, darling."

"I'm not looking for the ball," she muttered while searching frantically.

"Then what?" I asked, perplexed.

"My eye, it fell out." The game was put on hold so everyone could help look for the missing glass eye.

"I've got it!" shouted Naz, her friend who herself had only very little sight.

"How the hell did you manage that?" I asked with obvious surprise.

"I have to do it all the time," she answered nonchalantly.

Problem solved and the game was back on. Blind cricketers have many challenges to contend with but at least we never have to leave the field due to poor light.

I have to admit that very little happened after that. I was studying towards my masters and simply did not have the capacity to continue developing the team. I called the girls together and said this was their team and it would be up to them to grow it into something special. I am unaware if this ever happened.

With Blind Cricket South Africa I also got things wrong. I came back to South Africa guns blazing. I had big, bold ideas and was ready to explode onto the scene. But the scene wasn't quite ready for me. The organisational culture was also markedly different from what I had become accustomed to in the UK. I chose to take a step back to avoid any further conflict but I missed the game so very much.

Chapter 32: Running to Mauritius

Being back in South Africa was not at all the nightmare I had thought it would be. There were very many pleasant experiences and surprises, not least of which was the fact that I found love.

I do not like sitting around and waiting for life to happen. Not long after my return, I started looking into ways to meet new people, particularly among the gay community. The object was not to find love; that would just be an added bonus should it happen. There are gay dating websites in South Africa but not nearly as many as in the UK. I gave these a go but they did not produce the desired results. I met a few women online but the contact never turned into anything, not even a meet-up for coffee.

I did, however, find Facebook quite helpful. It has specific interest groups and I met a lot of people this way. This was also how I found a guide runner. I always picked good-looking women. Running isn't easy so doing it with some eye-candy provides a welcome distraction. Helen was one such woman. She was my guide runner back in the UK for several 10km runs and one gruelling half marathon. She was gorgeous and now lives in Peru.

I met Mandi on Facebook through another contact. We started chatting online and I loved it. She wasn't a runner but since we got on so well online, I invited her over one Saturday. My flat had a steep set of stairs to the front door. Mandi had not yet experienced my sneaky ways and so gladly obliged when I made the following request:

"Please can you go up the stairs in front of me, it helps me a lot?"

Of course I had no problem with the stairs: I use them every day. I asked her to lead the way so I'd have the perfect view of her behind. I fell hook, line and sinker for her. Mandi was much more cautious, though, and we started dating only six months later.

Wanting to spend more time with her, I asked her to be my guide runner at the next park-run. Though she wasn't a runner, she agreed. Our first run was at the Voortrekker Monument. We were nearing the end and I was doing just fine jogging behind this girl with the oh-so-yummy legs. I could see she was really tired and, of course, my wicked sense of humour took over. As we came close to the finish line, I gave her the bad news.

"We are only halfway Mandi, one more round to go." Even I could see her face drop. The Voortrekker Monument park-run included a massive uphill stretch of over 1km. It often brought even the best athletes to their knees. Doing it twice would have been absolute torture. I decided to put her out of her misery as I was struggling to keep a straight face.

"I'm kidding," I said, laughing. "The line you see down there is the finish." If she hadn't been so tired, she would have slogged me, I'm sure.

Mandi, as it turned out, was a natural athlete. That day, she did the park-run in just over 40 minutes. Now she does it in 25. She quickly became much faster and fitter than I was. We started entering 10km races and later even half marathons.

"Mandi you push ahead, I'll catch up," I said during a 10km race, completely out of breath.

"What about you?" she asked with sincere concern.

"I'll be fine," I assured her. I was holding her back and I hated it.

Since then I've taken to running with my cane. It's slow, it takes a lot of concentration and I've had a few accidents already but it suits me as I'm relying only on myself. Mandi always finishes way ahead of me, which is great because she can get the drinks and anything else we might need. I am not a natural athlete and running does not come easily. For some reason, I do enjoy it, and I guess the cane runner is here to stay.

We'd only known each other for a short while when I popped the question: "Mandi, do you have a passport?"

"No," she answered.

"Then we'll have to get that sorted because you and I are going places."

She looked at me quite puzzled but within a few weeks had organised the document. Travelling the world is great. Doing it with a good friend is brilliant. Mandi had never been abroad before and I wanted to change that.

Our first trip abroad was to Mauritius. It formed part of a work incentive, so our travelling party consisted of about 20 very excited people. The queue at immigration quickly put quite a damper on things. Mandi and I were up at 4am and she could hardly contain her excitement from the minute she opened her eyes. While she was standing in the queue, even her shoulders had begun to droop. I smiled. It was my turn to shine; I was going to put my magic powers to the test.

"Watch this," I whispered in her ear. "Stay with me but walk a few steps behind."

I started walking aimlessly, like an ant who'd just made his way through a puddle of whiskey. It worked. Soon an airport representative was at my side.

"Can I help, Ma'am?"

"Oh yes, please. I need to meet my bus for a transfer to my hotel but I have no idea what to do next."

"Please don't worry ma'am. Are you travelling on your own?"

"No, I am here with my partner and a work team."

And then the magic happened. We were whisked through security in no time. My white cane and I became the heroes of the moment. I have no doubt that everyone would have bought me a drink that day but it was an all-inclusive resort and a mere high-five and "cheers to the blind blonde with the magic cane" had to do.

Mauritius was a magical experience. Mandi is a ball of endless energy ready to bounce from one adventure to the next. She wanted me to join in everything. Although I was not always keen, I was determined to impress this fine young lady who was not yet officially mine. Water-skiing was on the agenda and I was more than a little apprehensive. You need at least some sense of balance and I had just about none.

Not that I would let this deter me. Simply attaching the skis to my feet was my first issue, and perhaps I should have stopped right there … Water-skiing looks amazing, but it's quite a cumbersome process. Once you've finally managed putting the skis on your feet, you're lowered into the water and given the water-ski rope and handle. The engine of the boat starts to rumble and slowly, as the boat gains momentum and the rope tightens, you lift yourself up and out of the water, the skis reappear and within a few seconds you're cruising along on top of the water with the wind blowing through your hair. If only. That process, from sitting on your haunches to where you glide like a Bond girl, is far more difficult than anyone would ever admit.

On my first attempt I fell backwards and skied (was dragged) like this for a few seconds while swallowing copious amounts of very salty seawater. The next three attempts were even worse. I went ass over tits and all you could see was my bum and skis intertwined. On the jetty, I had an audience of impatient brats waiting for their turn. My mood was going into the red and if those skis had not been attached to my feet (and really difficult to remove) I would have walloped the little scamp who kept saying, "Mummy this lady is stupid, will we ever get a turn?"

I was just about to give up when Mandi pleaded that I try one more time. The promise of the reward she whispered in my ear was not one you'd repeat in front of children. It did get me to give it one last go. This time, as I felt the boat start to move, I bent rigid, as though about to make a wee, and stayed that way until my body was out of the water.

"Woooo hoooo!" I shouted as I whizzed past the group who were clapping, probably from relief that my turn would soon be over. When the boat made the first turn, I came off and again swallowed a cocktail of seawater. The man driving the boat slowly brought the boat close to where I was floating in the water.

"We can try from here, ma'am. We don't have to go back to the jetty," he offered.

"Try again? Hell no! Home, James and don't spare the horses."

He got the drift and, with me sitting safely in the boat, we made our way back to shore.

"Wasn't that awesome?" Mandi said, full of her usual excitement.

"Dit was lekker maar dis nou klaar," I said, which means: It was fun but now it's done.

"But did you not like it?"

"Yes, but not enough to do it again."

Mauritius was magical at night. One evening Mandi guided me from our chalet to the entertainment area, then confessed that she'd forgotten the camera.

"Wait here, I'll run and get it," she said.

I waited and waited. Five minutes soon turned to 10 and after a while I'd been waiting for half an hour. I started to worry, but what could I do? Finally, she returned and, though it was dark, even I could see that she was walking with a limp.

"Did you go back to South Africa to buy a new camera?"

She was not amused.

"It is a full moon tonight and I wanted to take a few pictures for you with my special lens. I was in a hurry so I decided to run."

"You always run Mandi, even when you're not late," I interrupted.

She ignored me and continued. "I did not see a palm tree root and my foot got caught."

"Are you okay?" I asked, trying hard to hide my amusement.

"I'm fine, just a few scratches, but then it took me ages to find my lens cap and after that I also got slightly lost coming back."

I could no longer keep control of myself: I sat on the floor, laughing. Falling, losing items and getting lost are what happen to me regularly. When they happen to someone else, I revel in the humour of the situation. Karma usually bites me in the end but never soon enough for me not to enjoy the moment.

Chapter 33: Little Miss Mischief

Kelsey is my third guide dog and, by a mile, the most mischievous of the trio. While in a harness she's a star and works extremely well but when the harness and the lead come off, a little terror appears. Kelsey's trainer had told me from the start that she was a very intelligent dog, and that this would come with the very real possibility that she would also be very naughty. Well, Kelsey should have been called Little Miss Mischievous. One of her favourite devious diversions, for example, was to steal my towel while I was in the shower. And it wasn't a straightforward swipe and run. It was calculated. She'd wait for me to get into the shower, then make her move, swipe the towel and run. Then she'd wait for me to shout "Kelsey!" which she'd take as her cue. She'd answer me with an excited "Woof!", run with her head held high, my towel in her muzzle and leave it for me in the furthest corner of the garden.

Mandi had also fallen victim to the antics of Miss Mischievous. We'd arrived home after a shopping trip one day and Mandi was very excited about a new pair of running shoes she'd just bought. We went into the kitchen to enjoy a well-earned cup of coffee.

"What's that?" Mandi asked. "Is Kelsey ok?"

From the lounge we could hear little whining noises. What

Mandi hadn't known at the time was that that was Kelsey's tell-tale call to alert me that she was up to no good. When we rushed to the lounge, Kelsey was standing quite proudly with one brand new running shoe in her mouth. Before I could warn her, Mandi cried, "Kelsey!" And so the game began… She answered Mandi with a naughty "Woof!" and legged it, with Mandi running after her. Kelsey's plan had worked and soon an awesome game of chase was underway. I lost count of the number of times Kelsey and Mandi ran around the house before Kelsey finally let go of the shoe. Fortunately, there was very little damage to the shoe but from then on shoes remained well out of Kelsey's reach at all times.

Kelsey has now been my partner in crime for just over three years and is already a well-travelled dog. She's been on planes, trains and even a boat. She has visited all sorts of venues and done her fair share of park-runs. It would be fair to say I am now a seasoned guide-dog owner. I have learnt that the biggest challenge with every dog I've had has been the same. And it lies not with the dog but with the humans who cross our path.

Most guide dogs wear a sign on their harness: Working Guide Dog, please do not distract. For some reason though, most people seem to lose all sense and sensibility when they see a guide dog (for some people it can be any dog). People's first instinct is to engage and interact with the dog, and very often as though the owner was not there at all. I've lost count of the number of times people have approached my guide dogs and started talking to them as though I was not there.

When you do see a guide dog with its owner, please hold back and think. Would you do the same with a police dog or a sniffer dog at the airport? No! Why? Because they are working.

A guide dog is the same. First, please acknowledge the owner; it's called good manners. Then, if the urge to pet our four-legged miracles is really too much to bear, ask the owner. We don't bite.

Many years ago, before I had even acquired my first guide dog, there was a very funny Nando's ad on TV. It showed a blind man walking down a street with his guide dog. The pup smells the Nando's, forgets what he is supposed to do and follows the smell, leading the poor man to bang into a lamppost. I really thought it was hilarious. It was taken off the air owing to complaints which, I can tell you, were not made by blind people. The ad did, however, bring home the point that distracting a guide dog could be very dangerous and could compromise the safety of the owner.

Chapter 34: Gay Paris

Our next trip was to my second home, London. I explained to Mandi that we would be travelling to the UK. I gave her the budget and the dates but that was it – the rest of our itinerary was a surprise. She was under the impression that we were going only to London and Edinburgh, but I had other plans up my sleeve – Paris, the most romantic city in the world, and I was depending on it to live up to its name.

Visas would be a hurdle though. How do you explain to someone that they have to apply for two visas to visit London? Talking nonsense is one of my not-so-very-hidden talents. I contacted the French embassy and they were very accommodating. I told Mandi that we'd need to apply twice because the UK is part of the European Union and therefore we'd need one from the EU too. I also explained that they advertised for all countries in Europe, which was why there were posters of Italy and France everywhere you looked at the embassy. The staff was well aware of my plan and played along brilliantly.

Each time Mandi had to sign a form that clearly indicated France, the lady assisting us would cover the name with her arm and distract Mandi by telling her how lovely the UK was and all the things she had to look forward to.

At the British Embassy, we also had to declare our itinerary for our whole holiday. Again, I spoke to the staff and told them the full details of my cunning plan. They, too, played along. The gentleman interviewing us just said: "Wow! You're going to have a busy time."

I handed Mandi's passport to her and explained that one of the visas was for the United Kingdom and the other was for the European Union. I told her that France had been printed in there because it was their office at which we had applied. She fell for it through and through.

We boarded our British Airways flight. As usual, I had booked assistance as it does make life easier, especially at larger airports like Heathrow. As usual, I was offered a wheelchair and I gave the same reply I always do:

"Sir, the only way we will use this chair is if you sit in it, I push, and you give the directions."

You'd never offer a paraplegic a pair of spectacles, so don't offer me a wheelchair. But I don't mind using those annoying little cars that drive through the terminals. It is as though they scream: "Beep! Beep! I'm the annoying brat skipping all the queues. Beep! Beep! By the time I'm at home, you'll still be stuck in passport control. Beep! Beep!"

At arrivals, Des and Monique were waiting with our rental car. It was five in the morning and we were on our way. We drove for a while until we arrived at a railway station where our car was loaded onto the train. After some time sitting in the car while the train whisked us to our destination, we finally arrived. We disembarked and stopped for our first proper

Costa Coffee. Oh, how I had missed those delicious cups of Costa Creations of Excellence.

I said to Mandi, "Look at the road signs: do you notice anything different?"

She looked for a while.

"I have never been great at English but this is completely foreign to me."

Des and Monique burst out laughing.

"That's because it is foreign. Welcome to France."

I thought Mandi would faint. It was the 31st of December and we were planning to watch the fireworks at Disneyland Paris. Through Airbnb, we had found a cosy flat that was only about 5km away. We walked from there to Disneyland, since we'd already had several celebratory drinks and couldn't drive. We took a bottle of bubbly with us to see us into the New Year. When we arrived, we received the bad news. Our bubbly was not allowed into the venue and not even the impressive amount of flirting from both straight and gay girls could change the security guy's mind. Even my white cane lost its magic. Monique went to hide the bubbly but, as South Africans, we were very aware that the chances of it still being under that bush when we returned were slim to none.

We had lots of fun trying on all the funny hats, drinking mulled wine and watching the fireworks. When it comes to Disney, I have never grown up. I love all of it and, if they had let me be, I would quite easily have spent the rest of my holiday right there. My travel party had other ideas. We had to head back to our flat to continue our New Year celebrations. The big question was our bubbly: was it still there? None of us expected it to be and Monique was given the job to check. Lo and behold, not only was it there, it was perfectly chilled. Needless to say, by the time we got back to our flat, the bubbly was gone. Every last drop.

A certain amount of alcohol does lessen one's inhibitions and increase levels of braveness. Des came up with the outrageous idea of running topless down the double driveway in front of the block of flats where we were staying. It was not very busy but certainly not dead quiet.

"Not a chance," I said emphatically.

"First of all, I believe it is against the law and I, for one, don't want to spend the first day of the New Year in a Parisian prison. Secondly, it's freezing. Thirdly, the last time nudity was involved with you lot was when we - or should I say I? - skinny-dipped in Croatia. You took pictures and still taunt me with them when it suits you. So no, a definite no from me."

"But Tree," pleaded Monique, "we'll all do it together and no cameras, I promise."

My no was my no, until a mixture of more bubbly and home-made cocktails quickly morphed my emphatic no into a 'hell-yes!'. It is important to understand that, when it comes to the size of the assets that would be revealed by a topless run, mine would win first prize by a mile. The girls, although they are starting to head south due to age, are still pretty awesome if I do say so myself. My friends, on the other hand, had baps ranging from half tennis balls to Jelly Tots and an ironing board.

We stood under the not-so-flattering street lamp and, at the word go, ripped off our tops to expose our bra-less, freezing bodies, and ran like hell to the other side. My friends let me down. They did have cameras and they found a very dark area into which they ran, which of course I could not see. They said it was payback for me always taking the mickey out of them when it came to their boobs – or the lack thereof. I was guilty because I'd often said: "Any one of you could become my flat mate as you surely do fit the part."

Later that morning, with slight hangovers, we ventured into Paris. It was a perfect, cloudless day. It was cold, but it was a photographer's paradise. Once we reached the city centre, a common problem reared its ugly head. I just looked at Dee and she knew.

"Tree, don't tell me, you've got to pee?"

I was desperate. Luckily, since France is a First World country, ample provision is made for poor souls with tiny bladders, like me. We found a weird-looking public ablution. It looked like a little round house. I stood in the queue and tried to focus on other things while I waited my turn.

At last, the man in front of me came out. I could prepare myself mentally for the relief that awaited. As soon as he left, I dashed in, my jeans' button already undone, but the bloody automatic door would not close. There I sat with an audience blabbering in a foreign language. So I buttoned up and stepped out and, just before the door closed, dashed back in. To my shock, a loud alarm went off. Beep! Beep! Beep! With red lights flashing.

"This is ridiculous!" I thought. "I'm going to pee. Fuck the stupid alarm."

While I was in the process of relieving myself, the door opened again. Dear God, my audience had stayed for an encore. What could I do? I finished, washed my hands and left, but not without giving a little royal wave to my audience. Most people saw the funny side of this, except for one very upset and vocal French lady. She grabbed my arm and pointed to a plaque with finely-printed instructions. She proceeded to give me a very long and loud lecture in French, which I did not understand, but the word "bitch" came out several times. I lost my cool. I grabbed her arm and held my cane in her face.

"Can you see this? This means I can't read that," I said, pointing to the instructions on the plaque. "And if you can't get that, madam, you are the bitch, not me." I was warmed by a loud cheer from the crowd, who had by that time gathered around us.

Apparently these loos have a self-cleaning mechanism. Once one person finishes, the door shuts and the cleaning process happens. No one is allowed inside during the process. How was I to know? I should have read the instructions but my need was great. Like so many times before, my white cane saved my bacon.

Once my natural needs were taken care of and we'd all had a large, strong coffee to keep the hangovers at bay, the most important part of my plan was ready to be put into motion. We headed for the Eiffel Tower. When we arrived, Mandi's jaw dropped and she was speechless. The Eiffel Tower is just one of those places you have to see. No picture, movie or song can describe its beauty and the magical atmosphere surrounding it.

This is where I took my chance. Seeing that Mandi was under the spell of the romance of Paris and just about to comprehend the magic of the Eiffel Tower, I took her hands and looked into her eyes.

"I brought you here for a reason. I have known you for more than six months and I believe I have found the perfect place and time to ask you to be mine. So here, under the Eiffel Tower, on the 1st of January: Mandi Rudatis will you officially be my girlfriend?"

She said yes. I had played my cards well. Perfect place, perfect date and perfect temperature. The poor girl does not have a lot of natural padding, in fact, I don't think she has any body fat at all. She had to stay in my arms or freeze to death. Now that's what I call a result.

Chapter 35: Going mental

On the face of it, my first four years back in South Africa went extremely well. I loved my new job. I completed my master's degree. I became a homeowner and, in 2017, I was voted toastmaster of the year at my club in Centurion.

I'd been managing my mental and physical health well for some time. It was in January of 2017 that I started realising I might not have been doing as well as I had thought … I foolishly decided to ignore this feeling. I had suspected that after years of taking a particular type of medication, my body had become used to it and it had lost its efficacy. Though I was wary, I did not acknowledge the warning signs. Things were going so well at work and at home. I was winning many speaking competitions and other awards. My studies took up a lot of my time but they were nearing the end and that was exciting. At the end of May, I handed in my final thesis. A few days after this my world came crashing down around me.

I had been ignoring the warning signs for so long that my body did the only thing it could do, and I broke down both physically and mentally. As so often happens, the timing could not have been worse. Uncle Charl needed me at work more than ever before, but I could not be there for him. It was heart-breaking to let down the one person to whom I owed so much and whom I respected and loved.

One of my biggest fears came true and I was admitted to a mental hospital: Vista Clinic. I was scared. All the memories of the horrid hospitals I had experienced in the UK came flooding back.

My fears were soon allayed. Vista was nothing like any of them and one of the best differences was that they allowed Kelsey to stay with me. She stayed in my room with me and helped me find all the venues at which we had to attend seminars or participate in support groups. She was a huge hit with the staff and the patients.

The other big difference was the fact that the women on my ward and I all shared similar circumstances. We did not share facilities with drug addicts or potentially violent patients. Our days were very well planned and structured. In the mornings and in the afternoons we attended educational seminars and occupational therapy workshops. We were allowed to see our doctors every day. The ethos and philosophy of the establishment were clear: medication is not the only tool to help us to get better. Managing the way we live and think plays an even bigger part.

I don't wish a meltdown on anyone, but if it does happen to you, may you be as lucky as I was and be hosted by this facility. I would also advise such facilities to consider using therapy dogs like some hospitals do. The effect Kelsey had on some of my fellow patients was amazing. Just a few minutes of K9 cuddles went a long, long way to improving their day.

Mental health is an irritation to those who do not understand it. I thought my stay in Vista was very successful and most certainly the right thing to do. I came out ready to take on the world. What I did not realise was that my problems had not disappeared but had only been temporarily masked by my new medication. Deep down, the real problems were brewing and growing into a monster. I could have had access to the best doctors and facilities but, unless I dug really deep to find the source of my pain and fix it, I was never going to get better.

By November, I was struggling with severe depression unlike anything I had known before. I did not tell anyone. If I had, I would have had to admit the real problem to myself. It was a Saturday night in early December. I was alone and I did something that I hadn't done for many years.

I cut myself. Inside my heart was filled with unexplained anger, sadness and a desperate loneliness. The only way I could find any kind of relief was to take a blade and run it through the skin on my arm. As I watched the blood flow, I watched the pain flow away. I then tended to the wound in a gentle and caring way, the same way I would have loved someone to take care of the pain in my heart. It was so wrong, but for a brief moment, it helped. It did not last long. I ended up making six or seven cuts, all of which were cleaned and cared for in a kind and loving way. While doing so, I had a couple of whiskeys and I thought to myself, "That's enough." I went to bed but my head was spinning and working overtime. I needed more relief from the agony in my heart, the source of which remains a mystery to me today.

"It's Sunday tomorrow so I can sleep in," I thought to myself. But I needed to get my head to slow down so I took a sleeping tablet. I sat on the bed. "One won't do a proper job," I reasoned, and took a second. I lay in bed waiting for what felt like a long time. "Maybe one more would not hurt and then I can sleep it off tomorrow." Three became four and four became five. Finally, a sense of calm came over me. The pain in my heart had subsided and my head had stopped spinning. I was simply enjoying the peaceful quietude. Then an idea ambled into my mind. What if I could experience this state of calm and peace forever? That would be bliss: the choice was clear. I stood up, picked up the packet of sleeping tablets and took every last one.

This was my fourth suicide attempt. As soon as I had taken all the tablets, I began to worry. "It's not death I want, I just want the pain and heartache to stop." I picked up my phone and called Suritha. I knew her from Toastmasters and she lived nearby. I had just enough energy left to unlock the front gate. Which is where I was found.

I woke up in Midstream Mediclinic and was transferred to Vista, with Kelsey by my side. It was a week of great ideas and promises to get better. The problem was that I was still avoiding all the real issues. Unfortunately, my medical aid funds for the year had run out. I had no choice but to go back home on the Friday. I was not ready but I talked myself into believing that I would be fine. Mandi would be there to look after me during the weekend and then my brother André would come to stay with me to make sure I was okay.

I was back at work on Monday. I felt terrible and had to take frequent breaks to hide my anxiety and tears from the world. After work, I had an appointment with my hairdresser. I thought it would help to make me feel better. Later, we took Kelsey for a playdate and returned with a happy dog. We had a meal, after which my brother and his wife went for a short visit to his friend's place.

The house was empty and, in an astonishingly short time, the pain and loneliness clamped down on my heart again, bringing me to my knees. I immediately started cutting myself as I now knew it would provide at least some relief. I cared for my wounds, wrapping them up with tender care. I knew my brother would be back soon and I did not want to upset him. So I put on long pyjamas and went to bed, intending to pretend to be asleep by the time they returned. I thought about the sleeping pills and knew I also had some calming medication somewhere in my bathroom cabinet. I searched and found a selection of medicine boxes. I could not read the labels, but if I took enough, surely it would calm me down?

I don't know how many I took, but this time there was no chance to make phone calls or seek help. When I woke up, I was in Midstream ICU for the second time in one week. I was told that the tablets I had taken had had a bad effect on my heart and blood pressure. A tall woman with auburn hair entered my room and said she needed to discuss my situation with me and a family member which, of course, was my brother.

She looked at André with a stern face and said: "We have a serious problem here. Two attempts in less than a week. I strongly recommend that we transfer your sister to Weskoppies."

"What? That's for loonies, man! I'm not a loony!" I said, a little too loudly.

André gently put his hand on my arm.

The counsellor continued. "She cannot travel with you, we insist that she gets taken by ambulance. There is, unfortunately, a procedure that we need to follow. She must first go for observation at a government hospital and, in this area, that hospital is Kalafong." My body turned to ice and I started shaking.

When we were teens, a lovely woman called Vivian had worked as a cleaner in our home. We had loved her and she quickly became part of our family. It was a great loss to us when she died – attacked and set alight by her mother-in-law. She was in Kalafong Hospital and I clearly remembered visiting her. The horror of the place was permanently imprinted on my mind.

Now I would be going there. I was there for a week before being transferred to Weskoppies. My time in Kalafong was horrifying and the loneliest I had ever felt. I was the only white woman on the ward. I complained that I had not received my medication. They claimed that none had been prescribed but I knew this wasn't true. I asked to see my file but that was a big no, no. The nurses were furious that I had dared to question them. It turned out that I was right, but from that moment on, Kalafong became an even bigger hell for me. They often did not give me meals and regularly continued to withhold my medication. As a result, the panic attacks, which I had kept under control for so many years, came back with a vengeance.

I did not know where to find help as the nurses simply ignored my calls. I took a nail I had found on the shower floor and started cutting myself. This brought some relief. It felt like the panic in my heart became less and the care I took to look after the wounds on my arm made me feel like I was receiving the care I so yearned for.

This was my salvation, but it was very short-lived, so each

night, I repeated my healing act. Even with new, bloody cuts each morning, the nurses showed no interest. Dr Hitchcock, an elderly doctor, suggested that I just needed to breathe.

Each day I had a different doctor whizzing past, not hearing a word I said, and not paying attention to the increasing number of cuts on my arms. Finally, one young woman, Dr Venter, seemed to take note. I was given something to help with the anxiety and she pushed for my transfer to Weskoppies. Dr Hitchcock saw me again and this time she advised that, if I hurt myself or if I felt suicidal, I would be locked in the gated area where the uncontrollable patients were being kept.

The ward was one big hall for all psychiatric patients. One area was sealed with a black iron gate where a single patient was kept. She never stopped screaming and never stopped banging on the bars. Fortunately, I did not have to join her, but the threat of being kept there did nothing to help my anxiety.

A week after I had been booked into Kalafong, I was transferred to Weskoppies. I was crying with relief. When we were kids, Weskoppies was always known as "Loskoppies" (Loose heads), a place where mad people went and many a joke was made about it. Now I was going there. Life has a funny way of catching up with you, and the circumstances in which I now found myself reminded me of a quote I loved: "She needed a superhero so she became one." Even superheroes falter and blind pilots are bound to crash at some point.

"Loskoppies" was a step above Kalafong but only marginally. The food was bearable and my room was adequate. The first few nights were the same hell I had experienced at Kalafong. Again I was refused any medication to help me sleep. When I complained about anxiety and suicidal thoughts, I was given a stern warning: "If you are in that way," the nurse said, "we will have to move you to Ward 72." Ward 72 was a closed ward from hell. Patients were kept in their rooms for 15 hours a day, given a hard-handed bath by nurses in the morning and then left to fend for themselves as they shared a room with who-knows-what. The patients on my ward, some of whom had been in Ward 72, spoke with great fear of the experience. To avoid the nightmare that was Ward 72, I had to pretend that I was not suicidal and that I had no anxiety issues.

Once again, the only release I could find was to cut myself. I did so nearly every night but managed to hide it from staff and fellow patients. The only thing that changed was the tool I used and the extent and severity of the wounds I created.

Chapter 36: A glimmer of hope

I found out that I could ask to be discharged and moved to Vista in January, when my medical aid would kick in again. In the meantime, I had to survive Loskoppies. I had to pretend for at least two weeks by hiding the pain in my heart and the wounds on my arms. If I was deemed to be stable, come 2 January, I would be able to transfer to the safety of Vista. The day came: it was a Tuesday. I started to set the wheels in motion to get authorisation from my medical aid. Then my psychiatrist called me on the phone with news I did not expect.

"Theresa, we don't think it is safe yet to transfer you. Your psychologist said she believes you still have strong suicidal thoughts and urges to hurt yourself. We would like to wait a bit longer before you come to Vista."

Hours after the call I was still crying. I had to endure a third week of hell at Loskoppies. I guess this is where the final breakdown happened. The tears were endless and I felt weak and vulnerable, unable to hide my pain anymore. This finally prompted my doctor at Loskoppies to prescribe me a light sleeping tablet. I told her about my fear of being sent to Ward 72. She was shocked.

"This is not true. You would never be sent there for anxiety."

I can't blame the doctor for stepping in only when she did. I saw her only once a week and had thus far been rather good at faking my recovery and assuring her that I was getting better. I kept the truth hidden far, far away.

Although the new medication had been prescribed that Tuesday, I received it for the first time only that Friday, regardless of the fact that the pharmacy was on the premises. By then I was so weak that I had a break-down every evening when I was told it was not available. Again I was threatened with Ward 72. The incompetence of the nursing staff was matched perfectly by the state of the buildings. Though originally they had been quite beautiful, they were now in a state of complete disrepair. Some were even quite hazardous and a trip to the loo at night often meant having to dodge scampering rats. My list of complaints was endless, but I was well aware that I was one of the lucky ones.

My parents flew up from Cape Town and came to see me every day for two weeks. Friends popped in regularly. My cousin, Jax, visited me in Kalafong and several times at Loskoppies. She was a star, always ready to bring me what I needed.

The biggest surprise was my new writing buddy, Lynda. She had to travel quite far, but came to see me several times. She saw me at my worst. She listened, she cared. It filled me with a sense of calm that helped me through the last week at Loskoppies. It came from such an unexpected source and was so desperately needed.

I lost a few friends, or people I had considered friends up to that point. I do understand, though, that being confronted with someone who is struggling to deal with mental health issues isn't for everyone. If your knowledge is limited, you most certainly wouldn't have the tools deal with it, and that in itself can be daunting.

There was a mixed bag of women on this double-storey ward. I was lucky and had a single room downstairs. Most patients had to share a dormitory upstairs. Some patients had been there for months and my heart really went out to them. Was this the only hope in South Africa for people who suffered mental health issues but could not afford medical aid? Again, I realised how fortunate I was. Many of the patients had very little to look forward to, or even return to, should they be discharged.

My thoughts of suicide remained while I was at Loskoppies. It was only the method I planned to use that changed. Fortunately I never followed through on any of these.

Through all of the hurt and broken pieces, the support I was getting from family and friends gave me enough hope to hang on. We had long chats about how I felt and I started to realise that, although I could not see much worth in myself, to them it was clear as day. I also owe my life to some of the wonderful women with whom I shared a ward. They had helped me through some of the darkest nights of my life when I was more than ready to give up. On Friday 4 January, the medication finally came and I slept well for the first time in weeks. It made the weekend a little easier to endure. By Monday my bags were packed and I was ready to be transferred to Vista.

The doctor at Loskoppies suggested that I spend one night at home and then go to Vista the next day. I was surprised that she would even allow, much less suggest, this, but looked forward to spending some time in my own home. The doctors at Vista quickly put a stop to my plans and insisted I be transferred directly. There would be absolutely no stopping at home or anywhere else for that matter.

Chapter 37: The superhero you need

Vista was exactly as I'd thought it would be – bloody awesome! I was in a good space for the first time in weeks and for one reason only: I felt safe. I always stayed on the same ward, Disa. An angel called Morise worked here. She was a sincere soul who was passionate about her work. She was probably the biggest reason that I wanted to be there – she genuinely cared.

After a day or so, I went back to the ugly, angry, heartbroken monster. The reason: I was not dealing with my problems. Fortunately, by then I was under the care of my psychologist. She was a lovely professional and, with help from her and the team at Vista, I worked hard over the next two weeks to uncover the true identity of the monster so I could start fighting back.

The truth of the matter was that I had been lying to myself for so long. I was desperately lonely and had taken no measures to look after myself when it came to self-nurturing. Yes, I worked on my career and related interests, but never on me. The groups I attended at Vista were not always easy as they made me see the truth about myself and where I had gone wrong. I just wish, so very much, that everyone with mental health issues could have access to this information. The two classes that had helped me the most were on self-nourishment and stress management.

I always thought I was pretty good at managing stress. I often managed projects and events that could be very stressful. I believed I was proficient at time management after years of meeting project deadlines. I could not have been more wrong.

The class on stress management was presented by an occupational therapist contracted by Stander and Associates Inc. She first explained exactly what stress was and defined it as the body's reaction to external and internal stimuli that are seen as a possible threat. The result: an imbalance in the body. When the stress level is too high, it results in negative outcomes such as fatigue, anxiety and, ultimately, breakdown or burnout.

There are so many things that cause stress, some of which I was aware of, but others were internal stressors I had not considered before. Negative thoughts and poor self-perception are both major contributors.

These were also identified as the source of my depression. Over time, I had become prone to self-destructive beliefs. I always believed I needed to prove myself because of my visual impairment. I had also been convinced that it affected the way others viewed me. Combine these thoughts with not managing stress well over a prolonged period, and you will find that a very destructive monster of depression and anxiety takes over the body like a cancer.

We were asked to complete a questionnaire called The Stress Symptom Scale as found in the second edition of Stress Management for Dummies. A healthy score would lie between 30 and 50. The jury was out: mine was a very high 60. I was stunned. The presenter then provided a list of ideas on how to manage stress better. Guess what was at the top of the list? Self-nurturing. To be able to handle stress more effectively, you need to get to know yourself better.

During the session on self-nurturing, we learnt about the five love languages. These are words of affirmation, quality time, receiving gifts, acts of service and physical touch.

Another questionnaire was completed and it turned out that quality time came top of my list, followed by physical touch and words of affirmation. The fact that these needs were not fulfilled was one of the main causes of my illness.

The discussion of further tools to cope with stress was very informative. A balanced diet was discussed. Although not news to me, I did wonder about alcohol in particular. It was very hard, but I had to admit to myself and to my doctors that it could have played a part, if not in creating then certainly masking the monster. I never missed it when it wasn't available, so concluded that I couldn't possibly have a problem. But I was hiding the truth. Over time, I had fallen into the habit of having a whiskey or a gin and tonic after work when I got home. It was my little reward after a long day.

It was how I self-nurtured and it was toxic. It helped temporarily to hide the feelings of loneliness. Sometimes it took more than one or two drinks to keep the monster at bay. Alcohol is a depressant and worked against any medication I might have been using – especially antidepressants. Although it had felt like a good way to manage the stress, it was actually driving it to new heights. With my psychologist and my psychiatrist, I made the decision not to use alcohol alone at home again. This was not going to be easy, especially after rough days. I spoke to Desiré, Monique and Mandi and told them of my choice. They have been very supportive so I am hopeful that this will be one of the steps I can take, not only to deal with the monster, but to be rid of it for good. Exercise is nature's top antidepressant because of the endorphins it produces. This means the cane runner, who has been a bit quiet of late, needs to get off her ass and run more. I guess we will be back at a park-run soon.

Good time management is key in good stress management. I thought I was a professional at this due to my work experience, but I had it all wrong. I remember the presenter explaining the ABCDE method of prioritisation.

"A stands for very important – these are things you must do and, if you do not, there will be serious consequences.

"B stands for important – something you must do that will have only minor negative results if you don't.

"C stands for things that are nice to do but have no negative results if they are not done.

"D stands for Delegate – assigning it to someone else.

"E stands for Eliminate, whenever possible."

She then asked, "Where do you think self-nurturing should lie, A, B, C, D or E?"

I looked at the list and confidently said out loud, "C."

I was so wrong. It should have been A. Neglecting self-nurturing has serious consequences. I was a glowing example of this. I want to be the pilot of my life. At the moment, the monster is the pilot and it will take some time, hard work and the support of friends and family to chuck it out of the plane.

We should all be the pilots of our lives, not matter how challenging it might be. Once you are in the driving seat, don't take it for granted. Life has monsters in different shapes and sizes that will take over if we do not pay attention. If they ever do, please remember you are stronger than any monster – as long as you acknowledge what is there and not turn a blind eye.

As I write this, it has been four months since I sat in that small room in Loskoppies with my triangular glass weapon, cutting into my soul in an attempt to get rid of the pain.

Life certainly isn't a fairy tale and there have been many difficult days and even more difficult nights. The difference is that I now manage them much better. I've even let go of my stubborn pride and call for help when I need it – not when it's already too late. My time in Loskoppies and Vista taught me so much.

During this gut-wrenching episode of my life, I lost several people who I thought were friends, but I also learnt who was there for me. My mum, a very sensitive, broken woman herself, stepped up to the plate and, with my dad, supported me in every way she possibly could. My dad's values are based on Biblical principles. In him, unlike many others, it has brought out the best. Had it done the same for others, I'd probably have considered going back to our faith.

In this trying time, I finally understood what is important and what makes me whole. I need to, and can, make a positive difference in the lives of others – as I did for the lad who had

ADD. My current job is great, but I realise I need to make some changes if I want to affect more people in an inspirational and encouraging way. After doing some research, I have decided to return to London. I'd like to do my doctorate with a view to becoming a lecturer and assisting fundraisers and charity managers to have the best possible impact on their local communities.

Depression is a subject we don't talk about often enough. Not talking about it gives it strength. Talking about, and acknowledging it, diminishes the monster that takes over your mind.

If you told Facebook what you were thinking and put a message on your status that you had broken your leg, friends would come rushing to sign your cast. But what if you wrote that this morning you simply could not get out of bed, that your depression was just too dark to handle today and that it was getting the better of you? No one? Someone? Who?

There's this air of discomfort that hangs around the subject of depression. People don't know what to say to someone who is depressed or someone who is able to admit openly that they suffer from depression. More often than not, we don't need words and we don't need advice. We need a comforting ear and someone who is willing to listen and to just let us be.

I hope that through my experience I can help people be more open about mental health issues. Doing this is key to ensuring that we rise victorious against the deep, dark, demon: depression. Depression can be dealt with adequately only when we bring it into the light.

Printed in Great Britain
by Amazon

27042524R00138